STAR SG·1™

THE ILLUSTRATED COMPANION
SEASON 9

STARGATE SG-1: THE ILLUSTRATED COMPANION
SEASON 9

ISBN: 1 84576 310 6
ISBN-13: 978 1 84576 310 7

Published by
Titan Books
A division of
Titan Publishing Group Ltd
144 Southwark St
London
SE1 0UP

First edition September 2006
2 4 6 8 10 9 7 5 3 1

DEDICATION

For Brad Wright and Robert C. Cooper.

ACKNOWLEDGEMENTS

Firstly, thanks to all the *Stargate SG-1* cast and crew who helped put this together when you were also busy actually making the show! A special thanks to Michael Shanks for penning such a great Foreword, and Robert C. Cooper for the Afterword, as well as Dan Shea for his stunt diary. Many thanks to Bruce Woloshyn at Rainmaker for the fantastic pictures. Thanks to Brigitte Prochaska and Carole Appleby in the press office for setting everything up, and Karol Mora at MGM for your usual wonderful support. Last but not least, thanks to my editor Jo Boylett for putting it all together and kicking me when I needed it.

Titan Books would like to thank all the *Stargate SG-1* cast and crew, in particular those who kindly wrote pieces for this book. Thanks also to Bruce Woloshyn at Rainmaker for supplying the wonderful vfx images. As always, we're grateful to Karol Mora at MGM for her continuing help.

Did you enjoy this book? We love to hear from our readers. Please e-mail us at: **readerfeedback@titanemail.com** or write to Reader Feedback at the above address. To subscribe to our regular newsletter for up-to-the-minute news, great offers and competitions, email: **titan-news@titanemail.com**

Visit our website: **www.titanbooks.com**

Printed and bound in Canada.

STARGÅTE
SG·1™

THE ILLUSTRATED COMPANION
SEASON 9

Sharon Gosling

Stargate SG-1 developed for television by
Brad Wright & Jonathan Glassner

TITAN BOOKS

Contents

Foreword

Eventually all good things must come to an end. One has to close the book after the last chapter is read, thank the writer for the journey, turn off the bedroom light and close your eyes.

Or do you?

What does the musician do when the audience keeps asking for an encore? What does a performer do when the audience won't leave the theatre after the curtain call? I guess they do what *Stargate SG-1* did: you start again.

After four years of imminent foreclosure, and countless hours, year after year, spent writing the end to "the little show that could", Rob, Brad, John, Joe, Paul, Damian, Alan, Carl et al decided to do the unthinkable… stop stopping.

Welcome to season nine; a new beginning. With Richard Dean Anderson finally (and I do mean finally) moving on to bigger and better things, like life and the care of his precious daughter, we were all in a pickle. The godfather had passed the torch. Who would be there to take it?

With Christopher, Amanda and myself all there (when we weren't surrounded by mountains of dirty diapers and laundry), we were ready. We did, however, need some help to keep this boat afloat, and help we most certainly got. Arriving in the form of *Farscape* alumnus Ben Browder, Academy Award winner Louis Gossett Jr, Hollywood royalty Beau Bridges, my own precious wife (and *Andromeda* cast member) Lexa Doig, and the dearest touchstone of my career, Claudia Black. I think you would all agree: we filled the void.

And so marked the beginning of not one revamped series, but in a way two. Amanda, on maternity leave, could only join us by episode six, so we were stuck with a temporary gap to fill. In flies Vala Mal Doran (Claudia) with a scheming plot, a raucous adventure, and a catalyst that will shape the future of SG-1's antagonist-to-be, the Ori. Left in the wake of this reshaping would be all those adversaries that fans held near and dear to their hearts. Gone were the Goa'uld, the Replicators, and the Jaffa Nation as we have known them. Now we had a more sinister foe: a race of Ascended beings that had their own designs for the destruction of the recently acquired peace in our part of the galaxy.

Such was the brainchild of our writers: to create a fiercer antagonist for this stalwart band of seasoned gate travelers. An antagonist whose philosophies hit a little close to home for some religious purists.

Aww… why not?

Heck, we've spent years telling our audience that all the gods people have worshipped throughout history were nothing more than overdressed, oversexed, bass-voiced aliens that just wanted their thrones polished. Re-watch 'Seth' and you'll catch my drift. Why not tackle some not-so-obscure Christian myths? Well, there goes the mid-West demographic...

Trust me, we believe the long-standing fans of *Stargate SG-1* have suspended their disbelief enough that no one is going to start protesting outside the studio, or tomatoing our cars in the parking lot — Chris Judge would be pissed, and he's a large man. You guys who are reading this are not newbies to the show. You know that we often carry on with tongue planted firmly in cheek, so you'll know that offending anyone is not our intention.

What the "Boys at the Bridge" have done is carefully match out protagonists with a more than worthy antagonist. Because, let's face it, you're only as good as your bad guy in the TV world. Now your beloved characters find themselves in jeopardy worthy of their experiences.

Where is this new journey all leading? Well, I have no idea, you'll have to ask the writers. But I do have high expectations.

So, tune in: for the laughs (there are still a few), the friendship (it's all still there), the love (oh my god — who now?!), and the really, really big explosions (Martin Wood still drops by). We will continue to carry the legacy of what has become the longest running sci-fi series in North American history (I write to you from season ten — that's right, season ten — stay tuned). Our job has always been to entertain, to move (as we can do occasionally), and to be loyal torchbearers of the flame passed to us by Richard and by the fans that refused to let us end.

Fans, skeptics, critics, all those that thought we could, and those that didn't think we should, I leave you with these partially borrowed words:
"If we shadows have offended
Think but this and all is mended:
That ye have but 'tuned in'
Whilst we have 'begun-again'.
Now to 'scape the serpents tongue
I will make amends 'ere long."

How will all this shape *Stargate SG-1*'s tomorrow? To quote Daniel Jackson, "I have no idea." But it will be a lovely ride.
You keep watching, we'll keep gating.
Best wishes

Michael Shanks
June 2006

"The thing that's hardest to get used to around here is how good everybody is at their job."

No one, not even the show's executive producers, expected to work on *Stargate SG-1* for nine years. No science fiction television show runs that long — barring extraordinary phenomena with worldwide mainstream appeal such as *The X-Files*. For sure, the *Star Trek* sequels and spin-offs had led audiences and networks to expect a sci-fi show to run for six or seven years. But *Stargate SG-1* was already way past that and, since the conclusion of season six, at the end of every season the producers and cast had been prepared for the plug to be pulled.

Alongside its extraordinary longevity, a ninth year had other significant strikes against the studio deciding to renew, in the form of two huge cast announcements. Firstly, show star and executive producer Richard Dean Anderson revealed his decision that season eight, whether or not the show went ahead for another year, would be his last in the role of Jack O'Neill. Secondly, leading lady Amanda Tapping announced the impending birth of her first child, which, should a ninth year be green lit, would necessitate her absence from filming for a significant length of time at the beginning of the season. For a lesser show, the absences of two such huge names would certainly toll a death knell.

So, how do you make a show with two of its four main cast missing? Moreover, how do you continue such a show when you had just spent the second half of the previous season wrapping up every hanging storyline of the series' entire run anyway?

"'Reckoning' could have been a series finale, 'Threads' could have been a series finale, 'Moebius' could have been a season finale," reels off executive producer Brad Wright with a laugh, looking back at the final episodes of season eight. "'Citizen Joe' — that really could have been a season finale…"

Indeed, to all intents and purposes, *Stargate SG-1* had run its natural course and finished the epic story it had begun telling close to a decade before, in 1997. And yet *Stargate: Atlantis* had proved that there was an inexhaustible audience out there. The Stargate, as a prop, still had plenty of places to take viewers, in whatever galaxy the writers chose to open the wormhole into. There was really no reason to stop. The audience was still there, and the network revealed itself still eager for more. But how to continue when so many plot threads had been tied up?

Above: Cameron Mitchell (Ben Browder) learns the ways of SG-1.

For the producers, what could have been an overwhelming challenge in fact seemed like an exciting opportunity. "Brad said, at the end of season eight, 'Well, I think we've done it, we've absolutely ended the show in the best way we can,'" Robert C. Cooper recalls. He goes on to state, with absolute finality, "We're done ending this show! It was very creatively invigorating to be doing *Stargate: Atlantis*, because it was a beginning. Beginnings are much more interesting. You can only tie up so many threads. And I think we looked at Richard leaving the show as an opportunity. When the network didn't want it to go away, we had to make significant changes. We had wiped the slate clean by defeating the Replicators and the Goa'uld, and we needed something new."

"For a writer, change is fun," agrees Wright. "Change is a good reason to keep coming back. We don't want to leave this wonderful working line-up that we have. We love it."

The studio and network executives revealed themselves to be eager for the franchise to continue in some form, but still the problem of missing cast members remained. Both General Jack O'Neill and Lieutenant Colonel Samantha Carter were such key elements of *Stargate SG-1* that it was by no means certain that there was a show without them. In fact, in discussions about the possibilities, Wright and Cooper considered a very different avenue for the series. With so many main cast changes, the producers favored ending *Stargate SG-1* and launching an entirely new show, which would have been titled *Stargate Command*. Retaining Michael

Above: No, it's not a mirror universe — it's Daniel Jackson (Michael Shanks) and Cameron Mitchell.

Shanks (Dr Daniel Jackson) and Christopher Judge (Teal'c), the series would have moved on in its own right with new cast members and an altered objective while retaining the principles and writing style that had made *Stargate SG-1* so popular.

As it turned out, the legal complexities of ending one show and starting a new one in a similar vein proved too complicated. Instead, *Stargate SG-1* continued, though there was a little nod to their idea in the opening teaser of 'Avalon, Part I': as an awed Lieutenant Colonel Cameron Mitchell (Ben Browder) gets his first glimpse of the gate, Chief Master Sergeant Walter Harriman bids him a warm, "Welcome to Stargate Command."

So, having determined that *Stargate SG-1* would indeed continue for another season, the next task for the producers and writers was to come up with a new plot. Deciding on the basis for this altered series, which could so easily have been a separate entity to the original show, was of paramount importance. It had to tie into the ethos of exploration that had always accompanied SG-1's missions, which would allow the writers to make full use of Earth's most intrepid archaeologist, Daniel Jackson. It also had to recall the show's existing myths in order to provide a solid central role for the team's former Jaffa, Teal'c. But although both of these plot points had to be interwoven to provide a link between the old

Stargate SG-1 and the new, season nine also needed its own unique story. It needed something fresh to restart the show — something unique to introduce a new lead character.

Above: *Old friends... and new ones.*

Fortunately, this was exactly the sort of opportunity show runner Robert Cooper had been waiting for to explore a long-running story. "We had always talked about the fact that, if there was going to be some third incarnation of the series, or if there was a new series or a movie, one of the areas I wanted to explore was, 'Where did the Ancients come from?'" Cooper explains. "Atlantis was, 'Where did they go?' But what if they hadn't originated on Earth? That's where the concept of the Ori came from. What if the Ancients had come from someplace where they had left people behind, and the reason they had left people behind was they had philosophical differences. I was intrigued by some discussions at the time about how the line between science and religion was blurring. And although there are a lot of questions about science, I think there is also a new movement within the scientific community to suggest that maybe there is such a complexity to science — there is a higher power somehow involved. That was all just very interesting to me, and I thought that difference was somewhere at the core of the split between who the Ancients became and the bad guys they had left behind."

"Somewhere," Wright adds, "between both those sides of the argument,

*Above: The Ori —
a new threat to the
galaxy... and SG-1.*

two factions of beings were created that we called the Ancients."

The idea of exploring such controversial material as religion was appealing to the other producers involved in revolutionizing the ninth year of *Stargate SG-1*. One of those was director/consulting producer Martin Wood, who had been with the show right from its first year on air. For the director, establishing the bad guys for the new-look series was extremely important, and he recalls that there was much debate in the early stages of pre-production about what form they might take. "The whole season was completely different for everybody," says Wood. "It was introducing new characters and remaking it. New bad guys, in a big way, and making that a real threat to us. And you sit there and you look at it and you think, 'Well okay, how do we make a new threat? How many times has Earth been challenged? What is it that can challenge us now? We've got a good villain in *Stargate: Atlantis*, so do we want to bring that villain into our first galaxy?' That becomes problematic. The more you spread the villain all over the place, the less of a threat they become. If they have one target, Atlantis, that's a more immediate danger."

It was clear that the Wraith, though having proved an exceptionally successful baddie for the Pegasus Galaxy, would not be visiting the realms of the SGC for the ninth season.

"Robert really wanted to go into the new threat, into the Priors," Wood recalls, "using organized religion as a stump to work off of. So I think that was an interesting way to go."

Religion is a perennially difficult subject to cover without causing unhappiness on some side of the debate. But, as Cooper points out, *Stargate SG-1* has always been about religion. It has always highlighted the dangers of blind faith in 'gods', in the form of the parasitical Goa'uld. Introducing the Ori was no different. "I think it was a natural progression,

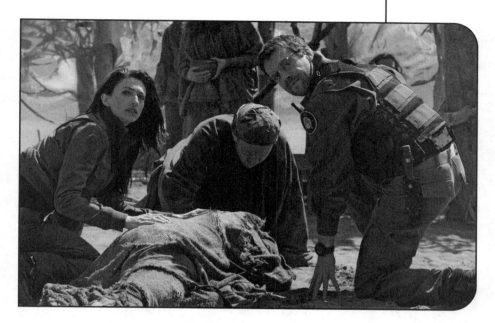

in looking for a new villain, to have something related to Ascended beings," says Cooper. "On the series we had always explored the idea of false gods and people's beliefs. We were never questioning people's religion, or God itself, but rather the actions people took in the name of those beliefs. [Introducing the Ori] was just a natural evolution, something organic to the series but at the same time new and very interesting."

The Ori were indeed a new concept in villain for *Stargate SG-1*, and therein lay even more controversy for the writers. The Ori, unlike the Goa'uld, are not 'faking' their powers; they do not use any obvious technology to control their subjects. They exhibit powers that generally could be considered divine. So who's to say they are not? "It's not like with a Goa'uld, where you can just kill the Goa'uld and say, 'Here, this is a piece of technology and here's how you use it,' and convince people that, yeah, that guy was just a charlatan. This is different."

Brad Wright agrees: "These guys are virtually indistinguishable from what could be called a real god who can actually manipulate the universe in ways we can't imagine!"

Still, Cooper insists that the purpose of the Ori is not to hold any particular religion up to ridicule or shame. The notion creates an interesting story, and provided an excellent starting point for jeopardy, which every good series needs to provide tension and interest.

Above: *Daniel and Vala Mal Doran (Claudia Black) see the 'powers' of the Ori at first hand.*

Above: Season nine had a distinctly retro feel...

"I certainly hope that we're not offending anyone with the invention of Origin and the Ori," he says. "With the Goa'uld it was a little easier, because you could shoot a Goa'uld and show people that there was a snake in their head. When we started *Stargate SG-1*, the Goa'uld were an all-powerful race that owned the galaxy. [They] had all these slaves and all this technology, and we had nothing. We started small, and we slowly built. We killed a couple of Goa'uld and got some technology, and then eventually we killed a *lot* of Goa'uld and we have all the technology that they had, and nobody is really a threat any more. If this is season one of a new show, how do you get back there? So, in creating the new villain, we take all those dynamics, all the things that have been *Stargate* in the past and just make it a little more powerful."

"We brought Merlin into it in a big way with the Arthurian legends, and that was a huge thing. The Ancients being split into two different directions is very cool," says Martin Wood. "The thing that hasn't been dealt with on *Atlantis* — and this is a whole other can of worms — is 'Ascension'. It's a nice tapestry now. Before, they were separate places, but now there are things that weave between Earth and Atlantis without having to take the Wraith and put them on Earth, and take the Ori and put them out in Atlantis. I think it's an interesting top-down look at how the

Stargate world works."

With the frame of a story in place, it was time to tackle the all-important, and daunting, task of casting the new *Stargate SG-1* line-up. "The beginning of the season was as much about introducing the characters, as well," Cooper points out. "We were eventually bringing three new team members into the fold."

The most important and most difficult of these new roles was a replacement leader for the SG-1 team. As the producers had experienced once before, during Michael Shanks' absence through season six, bringing a new face into an existing cast, especially one that had been running for so long, is no easy matter. To many viewers, Richard Dean Anderson *was Stargate SG-1*. Replacing him would be impossible, and in any case unthinkable. Instead, Cooper and Wright, along with their team in the production offices, created a worthy successor — and a character, it was hoped, that many viewers would identify with. Enter Lieutenant Colonel Cameron Mitchell.

"I felt the cliché was bringing in the guy that everybody hates and we slowly have to work around to liking, and his dark side is misunderstood, but he's really got a heart of gold," says Cooper. "I wanted him to be a fan, in a way. The fans were always going to have a problem with us

Above: *The Stargate — still the center of the show.*

fracturing the team. That was always a criticism over the [previous] couple of years — that the team dynamic wasn't the same, that we'd broken up the team. So I thought, well, what if Mitchell was a fan? What if what he really wanted was to get the team back together, only he really wanted to be on it. I thought that was just a fresh way of looking at his character and bringing in someone new. He's instantaneously a hero, [so] we could build his backstory into the show [gradually]."

Finding a face to match the character was less of a problem than one may imagine. The 'shortlist' of actors in Wright and Cooper's minds for the part of Mitchell was extremely short indeed. In fact, it only had one name on it — that of former *Farscape* star Ben Browder. "Now that we have him signed to a long-term contract," Cooper laughs, "I can probably tell you that he was the only one on the list! Obviously, the SCI FI Channel had a great relationship with him because of *Farscape*. Bonnie Hammer [SCI FI President] loves Ben and basically said, "Get Ben!" So we made him an offer. Our history with Ben actually goes back further than this. We had tried to get him for guest roles on various episodes, and then we even kicked around the idea of him for Sheppard for *Stargate: Atlantis*, but he was unavailable."

This time, however, Browder was not only available, but willing to dedicate himself to learning as much as he could about the show. Having played a role with huge cult appeal for a very long time on *Farscape*, Browder had first-hand knowledge of fan loyalty for lead characters. He was determined to honor that by investing himself completely in creating the character of Mitchell as a unique being.

"He actually watched all of the episodes," says Wright, shaking his head in amazement. "I mean, he actually sat down and watched *all* of them! It took him two weeks. He was in a dark room for a very long time, watching every one. We were stunned!"

"Ben was very conscious of not wanting to be perceived as replacing Richard Dean Anderson," adds Cooper, "and we certainly wanted to write a different character."

One of the ways that the writers found to show that difference was Mitchell's total enthusiasm for his new role, which verged on uncontrollable excitement. Certainly understandable for anyone confronted with the realities of Stargate Command's daily intergalactic chores, but, Cooper acknowledges, hard for an actor to balance against the necessary strength of a hero. "He kind of fought me, initially, about playing enthusiasm," says Cooper. "It's a tough thing for actors to do sometimes, because they are out on a limb. If they play enthusiastic and it doesn't work, then they just look like real clowns. No one wants to be the most enthusiastic guy in the room while everyone else is being sarcastic. It's tough. [But] he bought into it and made it work. I think Ben now looks back at it and thinks it was probably a good thing to do, but at the time he wasn't sure."

Having found the new leader of *Stargate SG-1*, the producers turned their attention to their other problem, that of covering Amanda Tapping's absence. The actress would bravely return to work six weeks into filming, just six weeks after the birth of her daughter. But until then, another character was needed to balance the team's dynamic. Sure, nowhere is it written that an SG team must have four characters, but for dramatic purposes, a three-person ensemble is difficult to put into action. Besides, another actress who had previously made a huge impression on cast and crew alike could provide a perfect bridge. Claudia Black, who had previously guest starred in the eighth season episode 'Prometheus Unbound', was thought to be an ideal temporary solution that would add a massive lift to the season's early episodes.

"Claudia came in and just wowed us on 'Prometheus Unbound'," Cooper recalls. "Amanda was pregnant and needed some time off, and Claudia came in and just took over. She owns the screen when she's on it, and it's so much fun to write for her. It's just like playing with new toys in the sand box.

"I think we'd be lying if we said we weren't concerned," Cooper continues, addressing the fact that the last time avid fans of television science fiction would have seen Black as a regular cast member was as part of *Farscape* — playing opposite *Stargate SG-1*'s new leading man, Ben Browder. Taking an acting partnership from one hit show into a totally different, equally well known one, had never been done before, and was another huge gamble on the producers' part. That it worked, however, is

Above: Claudia Black as Vala Mal Doran — *a different class of guest star.*

testament to Browder and Black's acting abilities, as well as the producers' intuition. Cooper shrugs, "I don't think anyone seeing them on screen together [in *Stargate SG-1*] would mistake them for Crichton and Aeryn Sun."

There were still more cast additions to come. General O'Neill's departure from SGC left the facility in need of a new commander. Enter General Hank Landry, an old friend of O'Neill's and a very capable soldier in his own right, played by star Beau Bridges. Casting Bridges was a coup for the show — and an illustration of quite how highly regarded the series had become in the industry. For Wright and Cooper, it was cause for huge celebration. "We sat around, and for a month or so we were like, 'Hey! Beau Bridges is on our show!'" Brad Wright laughs, "'That's *cool!*'"

With the casting now settled, the momentous ninth season of *Stargate SG-1* could forge ahead. For the show's regular directors such as Andy Mikita and Martin Wood, working with the first major new cast change in the series for the best part of a decade presented both new challenges and new opportunities. "I really love new characters, because for a director it's an interesting new thing to put into an old set," says Wood, "and watching them find their way is really interesting. They are so worried about fitting in with a cast that is so easy to work with.

"I had conversations with Ben, I had conversations with Beau and I had conversations with Claudia, [and] all of them said the same thing — they know they are coming into a meeting house where everybody knows each other and they are the new people. And when you go out to your ten million viewers, they don't know you either. They might know you from other shows, but they don't know you in *Stargate SG-1*. So everybody has expectations of you. I think as a director you have to juggle those expectations. The audience's expectation is this, the writer's expectation is this, the actor's expectation is this — so to tell this story, how do I do it the best way? That's really what it's about. So it's fun. When you go in to do a *Stargate SG-1* [episode now], the hardest part is figuring out the stuff that's in the script that's not standard fare. Those are things that everyone says: 'Oh, this is something new,' and they all grab on to it. Well, for the new people it's *all* new. So when you do a familiar blocking, they go, 'Oh, wait a minute, that's not what I would do.' That's when you go, 'Ah ha — the new thing!'" laughs the director. "Someone is not working in the same orbit that everyone else is. They don't have to, because they are going to show you what the new orbit is going to do with them involved. And I think that is truly interesting." Å

Opposite: General Hank Landry (Beau Bridges), ready to take command.

"General O'Neill gave me the choice of any posting I wanted. I chose SG-1. That meant Colonel Carter, Teal'c and yourself, not two letters, a dash and a number."

EXECUTIVE PRODUCERS:
Robert C. Cooper & **Brad Wright**

REGULAR CAST:
Beau Bridges as Major General Hank Landry
Michael Shanks as Dr Daniel Jackson
Ben Browder as Lieutenant Colonel Cameron Mitchell
Amanda Tapping as Lieutenant Colonel Samantha Carter
Christopher Judge as Teal'c

RECURRING SPECIAL GUEST STARS AND RECURRING CAST:
Claudia Black as Vala Mal Doran (1-6, 19, 20)
Louis Gossett Jr as Gerak (3, 6, 7, 10, 11)
Lexa Doig as Dr Carolyn Lam (2-5, 8-11, 13)
Gary Jones as Chief Master Sergeant Walter Harriman (1, 3-13, 15-18)
Bill Dow as Dr Bill Lee (1-4, 10, 13, 17, 18)

Avalon [Part I]

Written by: Robert C. Cooper Directed by: Andy Mikita	Guest Cast: Richard Dean Anderson (Major General Jack O'Neill), Martin Christopher (Lieutenant Marks), Tyler McClendon (Lieutenant Banks), Obi Ndefo (Rak'nor), Matthew Walker (Merlin)

Lieutenant Colonel Cameron Mitchell arrives at the SGC, ready to take his new position as a member of SG-1. Unfortunately for the colonel, he isn't so much joining the team as commanding a new unit with the same name. With O'Neill moving to homeland security and Teal'c returning to Dakara to assist with the formation of the new Jaffa government, Samantha Carter moving to Research and Development at Area 51 and Daniel Jackson requesting reassignment to Atlantis, the only current member of SG-1 is the shocked Mitchell himself. Mitchell tries to convince the old team to reform, but they're all adamant they have their own paths to pursue. Deflated, Cameron starts interviewing candidates, but is interrupted by the return of SG-12 with Vala Mal Doran, who has brought a stone tablet that purports to show the location of some "fabulous Ancient treasure". Supposedly located on Earth, Vala wants Daniel's help to find the treasure. She also has two "ceremonial marriage bracelets", one of which she puts on Daniel's wrist, the other on her own. The bracelets link them together — if they move far away from each other, they are both rendered unconscious. It's Vala's way of ensuring she gets her share of the treasure, and she won't remove them until they find it. Teal'c returns to Earth, and the team try to find the fabled hoard. Daniel's research suggests that one of the Ancients that returned to Earth from Atlantis was Merlin. He surmises that the treasure is buried in the mystical Avalon, believed to lie under Glastonbury Tor in Britain. Using a ring transporter, they beam into a maze of chambers under the Tor, empty apart from a stone block with a sword embedded in it. A hologram of Merlin appears, announcing that only those with a wealth of knowledge and spirit will be given access to Avalon's riches. Searching the tunnels in two pairs, both become trapped in separate rooms containing puzzles. They are being put to the test. Vala, impatient, fails the test and the walls start closing in. Mitchell also fails, and suddenly they're all in very grave danger…

Teal'c: Where is the rest of your team, Colonel Mitchell?
Mitchell: Actually, it's still just kinda SG-me.

The opening two-parter of *Stargate SG-1*'s ninth year would prove different than any other season première since its first year the best part of a decade earlier. In fact, the entire landscape of the series had changed so much that really the producers and directors were tasked with producing a pilot episode for an entirely new show, with new characters, new bad guys, new mythology and even a new galaxy.

"I certainly felt the pressure," says director Andy Mikita, with a wry laugh, thinking about the mammoth task he was presented with by 'Avalon'. "It was a big, risky event, as much for Rob [Cooper] and everyone else on the show as it was for me. The biggest issue was, basically, we were treating it like a pilot, but we didn't have any of the resources, money or the time to shoot it like a pilot. We still had to shoot it with a normal episodic formula — seven days plus one second unit day. So it's not like we were able to, from a production standpoint, treat it any differently."

Apart from the basic logistics of producing an episode big enough in scope to express all the changes of the year, Mikita was also about

Above: Mitchell gets to grips with his new role.

to put together what would become the new SG-1 team. There would be three major new characters entering the fray — Ben Browder's Mitchell, Claudia Black's Vala, and Beau Bridges' Colonel Landry, as well as Lexa Doig's recurring character, Dr Carolyn Lam.

"We had a lot of dances to do, especially with Amanda [Tapping] being pregnant and not having access to her for the first few episodes," says Cooper. "[But] just seeing the tremendous success of Claudia's character in 'Prometheus Unbound', we knew we had a lot of opportunities. And it's funny, in one review of the initial episode — I mean, we're nowhere near as smart as they give us credit for," he adds with a laugh, "but they said we were really smart because we didn't replace O'Neill with one character we replaced him with two, and that Mitchell and Landry are a combination of O'Neill."

Landry: No one's perfect, everybody has some sort of character flaw. What's yours?
Mitchell: Sometimes I can be impatient.

For Mikita, working with these new characters was one of his major worries. Had introduction of Ben Browder's Mitchell, in particular, not gone smoothly, it would have set a bad precedent for the rest of the season. "Ben was so well-prepared and versed," recalls the director. "He had watched every single episode of the show, which scared the hell out of me! I thought, 'Oh my God, I haven't even done that, and I've been on the show since day one!' He really did his homework, and that was encouraging. And both Ben and Claudia were around during pre-production, coming on location scouts and sitting in on production meetings, which I thought was very, very cool.

"Introducing new characters, sight unseen, was going to be a scary thing to do. So to have long phone conversations with Ben and for him to come to town early and spend a lot of time in the office to talk things through — we were addressing a lot of those concerns ahead of time, not having to deal with them while shooting. By the time we started shooting, we already had an established relationship, so we didn't have to cross that barrier. It was just, from day one, 'Let's have fun and see how it goes.' There was no new language to learn, we knew each other already, and that was great."

The producers had also developed a unique way of introducing the character — which, as Mikita puts it, wasn't so much actually introducing a new character as 're-introducing' someone the audience just hadn't

Above: Daniel struggles to overcome Vala's 'help'.

actually met yet. "He's kind of quietly always been there, we just had never met him yet," points out the director, "which I thought was a very clever way of introducing the character. And further, those flashback sequences just helped to provide some deeper insights into the character instead of just talking about them."

In fact, the scenes showing Mitchell's bravery during the battle with Anubis over Antarctica were some of Mikita's favorite parts of 'Avalon, Part I'. "Everything with the F-302 is great. Those [scenes] were tricky, as well, because we weren't flying exclusively in space. We had to have Antarctic sky out of the window of the ship. So from a production standpoint it was tricky, because we had to find some playback — they actually pulled some of the original aerial footage from the *Stargate: Atlantis* pilot, and we rear-projected some of those images outside the window of the F-302 and sped it up a little bit. It's kind of sketchy and unrecognizable, but in the end it was something to be seen out of the window that was not going to be a very costly visual effect, and so it had to be shot quite tight — you'll notice there are very few wide-shots, unless they were initial effects. But those were fun sequences. The whole experience was great." Λ

Avalon [Part II]

Written by: Robert C. Cooper Directed by: Andy Mikita	Guest Cast: Martin Christopher (Lieutenant Marks), Nick Harrison (Knight), Mark Houghton (Prior), Paul Moniz de Sa (Fannis), Obi Ndefo (Rak'nor), Stephen Park (Harrid), April Amber Telek (Sallis), Silya Wiggens (Therapist)

Daniel tries to solve their puzzle again, and succeeds. They are freed, but as Daniel rushes off to save Teal'c and Mitchell, Vala pockets a piece of gold revealed by the solved puzzle. Mitchell solves his puzzle, and they're all free. But even when Mitchell pulls the sword from the stone, and then defeats a holographic knight, the treasure is still elusive. Vala's theft is the problem, and once the gold and the sword are returned, the treasure appears. Daniel finds a book that describes the Alterans — the Ancients. Daniel wants to know where the Alterans went after returning from Atlantis, and a device found in the treasure trove may help. Meanwhile, Teal'c returns to Dakara to find that Gerak, whom he does not trust, is winning in the election. Daniel and Vala, still linked by bracelets, work on the device, which uses stones, seemingly for some sort of communication. Turning it on, they both pass out, finding their consciousnesses in the bodies of two villagers — Harrid and Sallis. The village is pre-industrial, and its inhabitants all worship the Ori. Daniel decides to explain who they are to one of the couple's friends, Fannis, who to his surprise believes them. Harrid, Sallis and Fannis are part of a faction of historians, a hobby outlawed by the Ori as heresy. The Ori are worshipped as gods, and Fannis describes their great power, but he hopes to be able to one day prove that the Ori are not their creators. Fannis takes Daniel to the burial ground to show him where the faction found the stones that Harrid and Sallis possessed. On their return, they discover that Vala/Sallis has been accused of heresy and challenged to prove her innocence in fire — she is to be burned alive. Daniel's protests go unheard, and the sentence is carried out. However, Vala is resurrected by a Prior, who arrives and demands that they both follow him...

Daniel: The universe is infinite.
Vala: No doubt it's deliberately ironic that we're in an ever-decreasing space.

The introduction of Merlin into *Stargate SG-1* mythology was an unexpected turn of events for established viewers, who had been watching the exploration of Egyptian myth for eight years. For new viewers, however,

Above: Vala pays
the price for not
worshipping the Ori.

it provided a perfect opportunity to become immersed in a new era of a show whose complex internal history had perhaps seemed too daunting to tackle. For the producers and writers, a new mythology meant new stories, a fresh approach, and a wealth of new history to explore.

"We wanted to put a new spin on this season. We just felt like we'd done Egyptian, we'd done Atlantis, so let's come up with some other thing," explains Robert Cooper. "It was like, 'Well, what if Merlin was an Ancient and that's where those powers came from?'" and it just snowballed from there. I think it worked perfectly, having Merlin be an Ancient. And I loved the idea of having a knight on *Stargate SG-1*! That was very appealing."

However, the most memorable — and talked about — scenes in 'Avalon, Part II' did not involve Mitchell's fight with the holographic knight. Instead, the striking image of Vala burning alive for heresy was what dominated the episode, both before and after 'Avalon, Part II' aired, and even before it was produced.

"One of the biggest concerns was the whole religious tone," recalls director Andy Mikita, "and how the audience was going to feel about dealing with religion in this way. Then, of course, that actual sequence, the burning of the 'witch' at the 'stake', had a lot of concerns for me, from a technical perspective, a safety perspective. It was really quite something. I was somewhat shocked when I first read it," Mikita admits. "It certainly implied that we were actually to see a person fully enveloped in flame, and [then] an 'act of god' bringing her back to life again in front of all these villagers. So there was a lot of discussion about that sequence."

Apart from the philosophical debate to be had about just how graphic the sequence should be, the production also had to tackle the practical aspects of burning someone in the middle of a set full of extras. "That probably occupied the most amount of time on the production for all of the departments," says the director. "Construction had to build a plinth that could withstand great amounts of heat, right on the set itself. Then the special effects guys [had] to come up with a means of pouring liquid fire down these channels and have it travel at a consistent speed, to make it safe for the actor. It was not always a stunt double. Ninety percent of the time, it was Claudia [Black] sitting in there with flames around her. So I had to plan those shots very, very carefully, and work with other departments to make sure that it was going to work and be safe."

Mitchell: So how are things on Dakara?
Teal'c: About as well as here.

"I love doing stunts," says Claudia Black, explaining her decision to get as close to the action of the scene as she could. "It helps the performance to be working with real elements. It was really hot. They just waited for me to pull the plug on certain set-ups, and they said, 'Go as long as you can.' I was breathing in a lot of that smoke! There's some coverage that ended up in the final edit, where you can just see that it's a wall of black smoke. I think we all suffered, our lungs were pretty full of it for a few days afterwards. But that was always my choice, and as I said, it can only help the work. I stayed in there as long as I possibly could, because I was aware of the shot that Andy Mikita was trying to get, and I thought, aesthetically, that it was just such a fantastic image. The way it's constructed, too — it looks like a maze, and you think, 'Oh well, by the time we get to the fourth act, she'll be saved just before it falls into the last pit.' And of course, that doesn't happen at all. She really does burn."

Though Black was willing to do everything she could to make the shot work in a practical setting, the production had worked out an alternative should the scene prove simply too dangerous to film. "The back-up plan that we had was a big overhead shot, finished with a lock-off," explains Mikita. "If things were not going to work out with the real fire, then the visual effects department were going to take over and we could always come back to that shot, but with CG fire. But fortunately we didn't have to do that. Hats off to our special effects department and our construction department, because they built a set we were able to use with practical fire, almost exclusively. It was fun, but for sure I had a lot of anxiety over the burn scene. When we finally ultimately

Above: *The amazing set for 'Avalon, Part II'.*

had to put a stunt woman into the middle of the pit and actually light her on fire — there's always a lot of anxiety [with that]. My heart was in my stomach when we finally did that. But Melissa Stubbs, the girl that we put in there, she does that for a living. And Dan Shea, the stunt coordinator, knew what he was doing, they had it all very well rehearsed and planned. Nobody got hurt and it all worked out great! It's pretty spectacular, that's for sure."

The finished article is one of the most effective and graphic scenes ever produced for the show. However, Mikita explains that despite this, the original cut was even more shocking. "The original cut was far more graphic. I just thought that the way we [had] shot the material, there was only one way to go about it — go big, or forget about it. Then Robert [Cooper] cut it back to where he felt comfortable with it.

"I'm very pleased," Mikita continues, about the episode as aired. "I thought Michael Shanks did an extraordinary job with it, as did Claudia. They both exceeded my expectations. I'm their biggest fan, and Michael never ceases to amaze me with what he is capable of. With Claudia, the more you work with her, the more you realize what she is capable of. So I was very pleased." Λ

Origin

Written by: Robert C. Cooper
Directed by: Brad Turner

Guest Cast: Richard Dean Anderson (Major General Jack O'Neill), Penelope Corrin (Dr Lindsay), Julian Sands (Doci), Greg Anderson (Administrator/Prior), Mark Houghton (Prior #1), Larry Cedar (Prior #2), Stephen Park (Harrid), April Telek (Sallis), Paul Moniz de Sa (Fannis), Gardiner Millar (Yat'yir)

Daniel and Vala are taken to the planet of Celestus. Back at the SGC, their bodies are being monitored and are currently stable, though Landry orders Lam to take steps to disconnect them if they go into shock again. A Prior has arrived on another planet, and Mitchell takes SG-12 to witness his 'miracles' for themselves. Meanwhile, Daniel asks for an audience with the Doci, who appears to have plenty of foreknowledge about the archaeologist. He repeats that all those who do not serve the Ori will die. Back at Stargate Command, Gerak, a powerful leader amongst the Free Jaffa, arrives to discuss terms of treaty with Landry. He does not seem particularly eager to make friends with the *Tau'ri*. Mitchell and SG-12 talk to the Prior, who is aware of Daniel's visit to their galaxy. Daniel, meanwhile, refuses to accept that the Ori are gods or that the Priors worship them willingly. The Doci appears to take on the characteristics of the Ori themselves, and a voice asserts that the Ori will demonstrate their powers. Gerak is still at Stargate Command when Mitchell arrives with the Prior. Daniel and Vala are returned to the village, where the Prior has said a "cleaning" will take place. Daniel thinks the artifacts uncovered by Fannis could hold the key to defeating the Ori. Fannis takes them to another communication device, and using it means Daniel and Vala begin to wake up at SGC — but then the Prior arrives, shutting down the device and killing Fannis. Daniel and Vala are tried again, and their 'real' bodies again begin to die. Mitchell has the idea of gating the device out of SGC. Doing so breaks the connection, and they wake up. The Doci, meanwhile, promises to build a fleet of "Godships" to attack the unbelievers...

Daniel: This is bad.
Vala: Worse than being burned to death?

'Origin', as an episode, was actually never intended to exist in its own right. However, as executive producer Robert Cooper worked on the opening episodes of season nine as an introduction to a whole new *Stargate SG-1*, it

Opposite: Mitchell and a visiting Prior.

became apparent that more was needed for the story than what has been created for 'Avalon'. "It was originally a two-parter," explains Cooper of the season opener. "When we boarded the story, we only focused on the story beats. But, as I got into the script, I realized there were so many character beats that needed to be explored. I made it a three-parter after writing the first hour, because I felt the first episode needed to be about the characters and less about plot."

This change — the addition of a further episode in the mini-arc that opened the season — meant much more work for Cooper, both as executive producer and as writer on the first three episodes. Cooper confesses, however, that it was the latter role that proved the biggest challenge. "It was more taxing on me as a writer," he admits. "I really felt a lot of pressure to introduce new characters and set up the new bad guys, the Ori."

The writer's work in introducing the Ori would later prove to be controversial. When the season aired, some viewers saw the Ori's fanaticism and use of religion as a tool of power as an accusatory look at organized religion in the Western world.

Prior: Lessons of days gone by teach us of what will come to pass.
Mitchell: I'm a bit of a history buff myself. Doesn't help me pick the lotto numbers, though. So, where you from?

"The Ori are really sinister," he agrees. "*Stargate SG-1* has always been controversial, and I'm surprised that people are suddenly starting to notice. I guess we've gotten really close to modern day hot topics. We've been accused in the past, too, with [season three episode] 'Demons'. 'Demons' was a thinly veiled allusion to Catholicism. But the Ori are not a criticism or indictment of any one religion. People have chosen to interpret it that way. Others have defended it as, correctly, a comment on the evils of *all* religions. Where does religion go wrong? Why is extremism a problem? That's obviously something that everybody can relate to. We've always felt that our show, [being] science fiction, has been an opportunity to explore those ideas in a slightly more fantastic form."

'Origin', besides examining in further depth the Ori and their plans for their followers, also introduced another character that would recur throughout the first half of the season. Academy Award winner Lou Gossett Jr arrived to play the role of Gerak, a key figure in the ongoing story of the Free Jaffa Nation's move towards democracy.

"Lou was actually being discussed to play General Landry," Cooper reveals. "It never dawned on us that we'd have both Lou and Beau want to do the show! It was an embarrassment of riches. In the end, it worked out for Beau to play Landry, and we created the Gerak character for Lou. He seemed to like the idea of playing a complicated bad guy."

Continuing along the theme of character introductions, 'Origin' also wrapped up the integration of Colonel Cameron Mitchell into Stargate Command and his position as leader of SG-1. What better way to solidify that new role than with a 'hand over' from the former star of the show, Richard Dean Anderson?

Above: The embarkation room — fully secure.

Though the former executive producer had stepped away from the show entirely, he agreed to appear in a charming final scene with new star Ben Browder. "I wrote those scenes only after I knew RDA had agreed to be in the show," says Cooper. "I struggled a bit over what the last scene between Mitchell and O'Neill should be. It seems so clear now, in hindsight, that helping Mitchell get back on the horse and fly an F-302 again is the perfect gesture for O'Neill to make."

Despite, or maybe even because of the later controversy that would surround the introduction of the Ori, one of the aspects that most pleased Cooper about the finished episode was the appearance of SG-1's new arch-nemeses. "I wanted the Priors and the Doci to be creepy and scary. They are the face of the new villains, and I think they definitely come off that way — in large part because of Joel Goldsmith's fabulous score."

Though it was written as an addition to the original two-part story, Cooper reveals that a substantial chunk had to be removed from the final edit. "In fact, there was almost eleven minutes lifted for time and pacing but nothing that I would put back," he says. "There were a few beats that dealt with Landry and his daughter Dr Lam's relationship that didn't make it, but the arc of their story is still there. Also, you always end up losing dialogue when the visuals work. When you don't need it to tell the story it's always better to let the scene play. The final burning sequence had more talking in it, but it seemed to just break the tension. It played much better with just the action." Λ

The Ties That Bind

Written by: Joseph Mallozzi &
Paul Mullie
Directed by: William Waring

Guest Cast: Morris Chapdelaine (Tenat), Bruce Gray
(Senator Fisher), Darren Moore (Vosh), Michael P. Northey
(Inago), Eileen Pedde (Major Gibson), Geoff Redknap
(Jup), Malcolm Scott (Caius), Wallace Shawn (Arlos)

Vala leaves Earth, but an hour later, Daniel passes out — the effect of the cuffs still hasn't worn off. Returning, Vala admits there is someone who might know about the side effects of the bracelets... the person she stole them from. The said scientist, Arlos, says he's never heard of the bond lasting beyond the bracelets being taken off, though he might be able to help, but not until a necklace Vala stole from him is returned. It's unlikely they'll be able to find it again, but they don't have much choice. They visit a Jaffa trader, Inago, but discover that Vala left yet another mess behind her in her dealings with him. He won't give the necklace back unless Vala returns an obsolete power coil he sold her. Which, unfortunately, she sold on to a group of monks, by convincing them it was a religious relic of great importance. The 'monk' she gave it to is actually a smuggler in hiding and he needs the cargo ship Vala 'borrowed' from him years before — or no power coil. Unfortunately, the ship is now the property of the Lucian Alliance, who want Vala and Daniel dead after their last encounter. Landry won't authorize them taking the ship by force, so for the time being they're stuck together. Landry tells them to prepare for a trip to Washington, where he needs Daniel to help convince the Appropriations Committee that SGC must keep their current budget, which is under threat. Daniel tries to work, with Vala buzzing in his ear, but the meeting with the Appropriations Committee does not go well, and Vala makes it worse. Landry, outraged, orders SG-1 to go after the ship. They have to get rid of Vala! Mitchell and Teal'c pretend they have Vala and Daniel as prisoners in order to infiltrate the ship, which works. They return to Arlos, having regained his necklace — only to be told that the effect of the bracelets will eventually wear off naturally.

Vala: I hate long goodbyes.
Jackson: Okay, goodbye.

Season nine of *Stargate SG-1* deliberately struck out to present a new type of episode to both the new and existing audience, and 'The Ties That Bind'

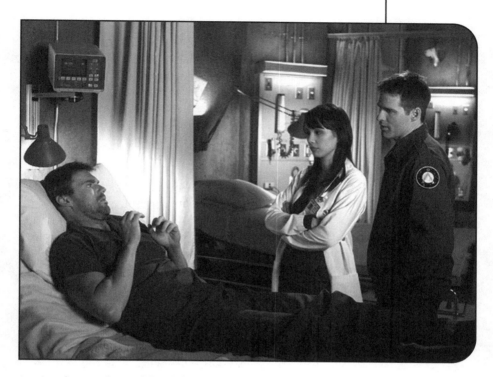

Above: *Lexa Doig (Dr Carolyn Lam) acts in a scene with her husband, Michael Shanks.*

in particular is evidence of this shift in style.

"'Ties That Bind' is not a typical *Stargate SG-1* episode," agrees executive producer Robert C. Cooper. "I sat down with each of the directors and said, 'I don't know if there is a perceived rule book about how to make *Stargate SG-1*, but I think we should throw that out this year. And maybe shoot the shows differently, too.' I think the episodes do have a different look. There's a different look and feel, and there were times that people would say, 'Well, that's not *Stargate SG-1*.' But in a way, I think that's good."

'The Ties That Bind', apart from anything else, gave viewers a longer glimpse into the past of Vala Mal Doran — a glimpse that for the most part confirmed prior suspicions about her frequently unorthodox business dealings! Taking a character that has previously appeared as a guest and fleshing them out into a full creation for the screen can be tricky. A guest character often has more leeway than a character being introduced as a recurring or regular feature of the series, and so it might have been necessary to tone down Vala in readiness for her temporary, if extended inclusion in the SG-1 team. Executive producer Joe Mallozzi, however, who took the lead in penning the script for 'The Ties That Bind', reveals that writing for Vala could not have been easier. "I would say that that's perhaps one of the easiest scripts I've ever written," Mallozzi says with a laugh. "It was a lot of fun, and I love the character. It also gave us an opportunity to introduce other rogue elements, like the pirates and the Jaffa, that were just so much fun to write. Whenever we get an opportunity to do humor, we embrace it. More often than not, it's little flashes of humor within serious episodes, but on occasion we get to write a wholly comic episode, and this was one of those. And it was one that I embraced and it was a fairly easy write."

Teal'c: There are times you remind me of O'Neill.
Mitchell: I'll take that as a compliment.

However, for Claudia Black, who was getting used to playing a fuller version of Vala than she had previously had a chance to explore, some aspects of the episode didn't quite chime with her own thoughts about the character. "[There was] a scene that was cut in 'Ties That Bind', with Wallace Shawn (Arlos). Joe Mallozzi and Paul Mullie had written that Vala had slept with his character, had had an affair. I went to Rob [Cooper] and I said, 'Is this really who you see Vala as? You really see her as a girl who is talking about it all the time, but is also actually *doing* it? That she doesn't discriminate?' And he said, 'No, I don't see her like that at all — I think that's just something that the boys threw in.' I just didn't see her being that way. I believe that she does have a moral vein in her body, and those that talk about it all the time are probably not getting any!" Black laughs. "So there was a scene [added] where we're in the bar, where Daniel and Cameron come back and say, 'We can't believe you did that to him!' and she says, 'Oh, come on, I got him drunk and let him think what he needed to think.' That, to me, was an important scene to show how Vala operates. I don't think she would deliberately manipulate people physically. But it got cut, and so there's a scene where he says they were lovers and there's no scene on screen where she rebuts it. But that happens. The gods of timing will always interfere!"

In actual fact, that scene wasn't the only one to be lost from the final episode, as Mallozzi explains. "At times it's just a mystery as to why some scripts go long and some scripts are short. In 'Ties That Bind' we had to cut scenes just for time. A bar room scene at the end of the first act, where it's Mitchell and Daniel dragging some poor sod out of the tavern, and Vala's checking her bruised knuckles, implying

that she took him out! They question Vala about what Arlos has told Daniel about her and Arlos and their carnal relationship. The other scene was a Teal'c scene where he comes through the gate and meets Mitchell, and they discuss Mitchell's search for a replacement for Teal'c. And basically he's mentioning it to Teal'c as a way to prod him, perhaps, into coming back. But Teal'c doesn't bite. And the other scene is one that I'm sorry we lost. It's an exchange between Mitchell and Tenat. Mitchell goes off on a little riff explaining the types of villains he's tracked down."

For Mallozzi, it's an episode he has fond memories of writing and producing, and he highlights in particular the work of the guest talent. "Not enough can be said about how a guest star can make or break an episode," he explains. "It's tough when you're writing a comic episode, because if the timing isn't there, it'll fall flat — and everything revolves around the comedy. If that doesn't work, then the episode is a disaster. In this case, I thought the guest stars were terrific and they worked really well. Also, the dynamic between Mitchell, Daniel and Vala that we establish in this episode is a lot of fun. Hopefully that set the tone for their future relationship." Å

Above: The 'new' *SG-1.*

The Powers That Be

| Written by: Martin Gero | Guest Cast: Greg Anderson (Prior), Cam Chai (Azdak), |
| Directed by: William Waring | Pablo Coffey (Vachna) |

Vala is still very much resident at Stargate Command, much to the irritation of Mitchell and Jackson. However, when she says she has a good relationship with one of the planets reported to have recent Prior activity, it seems sensible to use her information while checking the planet out. However, SG-1 soon discover that Vala's 'good relationship' with the people of P8X-412 results from her days as a host of the Goa'uld Qetesh — a queenly role she wasn't above continuing even after the Goa'uld was removed, thanks to a voice synthesizer and Goa'uld-like costume she dons once again upon arriving at the planet. As 'Qetesh' Vala asks the villagers about their recent Prior visitor. It's soon apparent that the people are divided over who to worship — their old goddess or the Prior. Daniel persuades Vala to reveal her true identity in a bid to prove to the villagers that gods do not exist and they should no more worship the Ori than they should the Goa'uld. Unfortunately this plan backfires, as the villagers are outraged and insist on putting Vala on trial for all the crimes committed by Qetesh. During Daniel's defense of her, the Prior arrives and argues with him about the nature of divinity and responsibility. The Prior issues an ultimatum to the people — serve the Ori or die. Leaving them to think it over, he 'proves' his power by making the villagers sick. Daniel and Vala attempt to cure them using a healing device, but the people simply relapse — and Mitchell soon falls ill too. The Prior returns, and in return for their worship of the Ori, heals the villagers, even bringing one back from the dead. The Prior leaves, warning Daniel to tell all of what he has seen.

Vala: Don't you care that there could be Priors out there taking advantage of poor innocent people, luring them into an oppressive religion or worse... killing them for rejecting it?
Mitchell: Are you bored of bothering Jackson?

'The Powers That Be' marked a milestone for writer Martin Gero, as the *Stargate: Atlantis* writer penned his first episode of the parent show for season nine. "I was not in a position to work on *Stargate SG-1*," says Gero, of his first year as part of the production team. "You can come onto *Stargate: Atlantis* because it's new and you have to just be familiar with the format more than anything. But after being around for a year, I'd been soaking

Opposite: Daniel discovers that old habits die hard for Vala.

it all up and watching season eight of *Stargate SG-1* — and we just decided it was kind of ridiculous not to work on both shows. I pitched an idea that I thought would be fun for Vala's character. Rob [Cooper] liked it, and we fleshed it out a little bit. So that's how that came about. At a certain point, Rob had to take the script over because I had gone back to *Stargate: Atlantis*. But some of the funnier stuff is mine!" he promises with a laugh. "I essentially wrote the first half of it and Rob had a stronger hand in the second half."

Gero's story allowed the show to explore more of Vala's sketchy past, as well as furthering the encroachment of the Ori threat into our galaxy. For actress Claudia Black 'The Powers That Be' allowed her to give more of an insight into her character. "It's interesting, because you're obviously seeing a part of Vala's past," says Black. "You're getting into contact with people who have had to deal with her before. She is, I think, a loveable rogue, but in terms of morality she learns a valuable lesson. She realizes her part in things."

Despite this acknowledgement of Vala's somewhat morally dubious choice in masquerading as a Goa'uld, the actress feels her character's manner is still largely simply misunderstood. "I don't think you entirely blame her, because it's always been about survival for her. She's always had to be on the run, and I don't know if that's always been entirely her fault. The first time she had to run away, it might not have even been her fault and she's had to be on her toes ever since."

Vala: I'm pleading innocent, right?
Daniel: You already confessed!
Vala: A god can change her mind, can't she?

Writer Martin Gero explains that one of the challenges of writing the episode was how early it came in season nine. With all the changes that had occurred since season eight went off air, getting the nuances of the 'new' *Stargate SG-1* right took time, particularly when it came to big bad guys the Ori, and the scene in which Daniel Jackson goes head to head in debate with a Prior. "The final draft of 'The Powers That Be' was actually written at the same time as the first draft of episode three," he explains. "Because 'Origin' hadn't been written yet, I kind of wrote the first draft of it without really knowing much about the Ori, because we hadn't figured it out yet! So that big trial sequence went through a lot of changes once we figured out what the deal was."

The same scene also caused various issues for director Will Waring,

though for more practical reasons. "One of the challenges for me in that script was the whole trial scene,'" he says. "Pages and pages and pages that all take place in the same set — you want to keep it visually interesting, so it's really hard to shoot."

Above: The SG-1 boys refuse to take "no" for an answer.

To avoid the possibility of repeating a shot, Waring devised a lighting method that could be changed for every shot, subtly altering the atmosphere as the camera angle moved. Pre-setting all the lights, Waring chose a principle direction in which to shoot. After filming a block of scenes at that angle, he moved the camera slightly and changed which lights were turned on, so that it not only looked as if it was filmed in a different location, it also looked as if it was filmed at a different time of the day.

Another challenge to overcome was the basic logistics problem of shooting a scene with a lot of people — or at least, a scene that needs to look as if it involved a lot of people! "The big challenge in a scene like that is you're supposed to have a crowd of fifty people," explains the director, "and fifty people are really expensive to keep around for that length of time. So I think we had twenty-five. You have to shoot them in a way that it looks like fifty — but there are a lot of character faces in there where you could say, 'Hey! That guy was standing behind in that last shot!' So we really had to pay attention to that. So we put *this* face in the background and maybe we'll put the hood up a little higher. We paid very close attention and I don't think you'll find the same face in two directions!" Å

Beachhead

Written by: Brad Wright
Directed by: Brad Turner

Guest Cast: Donald Adams (Latal), Eileen Barrett (Birra), Ian Butcher (Prior), Maury Chaykin (Nerus), Martin Christopher (Lieutenant Marks), Barclay Hope (Colonel Lionel Pendergast), Dan Shea (Sergeant Siler)

Prior appears on Kalana, killing the Jaffa population and raising a shield around himself and the gate. At SGC, a Goa'uld named Nerus arrives, revealing that the forcefield will allow the Ori to bring through armies from their own galaxy. It has also kept the gate open for more than two days. Nerus offers to help. Landry recalls Sam Carter, and the team depart to Kalana aboard the *Prometheus*. Carter has a new weapon to use, at O'Neill's insistence, though she doesn't believe it will be enough. Nerus recommends that they bombard the gate with nuclear weapons, but Landry wants them to talk to the Prior first. They take with them Carter's 'gatebuster', a naquadria-enhanced nuclear bomb. Mitchell warns the Prior that they will detonate the weapon if the Prior does not shut the gate down in thirty minutes. The Prior ignores them, and the team are still on the planet when Gerak's Jaffa arrive in orbit and begin to bombard the forcefield. The shield not only holds, it expands. SG-1 return to the *Prometheus* and the gatebuster detonates, further expanding the forcefield to encompass the entire planet. Gerak continues to fire, but Carter realizes that their fire is helping the Ori. She surmises that they are planning to implode the planet, creating a black hole that could power a Supergate. The planet is a beachhead, and Nerus is working for the Ori. The gate on Kalana starts to bring through parts of a huge gate that begins to form in orbit around the planet. Vala hijacks one of the Jaffa cargo ships and flies it into the still-forming gate, planning to disrupt the chain holding the pieces together and hoping to transport back before the resulting unstable wormhole forms. The Supergate is destroyed, but she doesn't make it back. The Ori have been thwarted, but SG-1's odd extra member is lost, possibly in the Ori galaxy…

Jackson: Vala, this is a military vessel.
Vala: I know, darling, I've stolen it before.

Having spent the first five episodes of the season talking about the threat of the Ori, it was time to see their armies do their worst yet — namely, attempt to launch a full-scale attack on our galaxy. "'Beachhead' came out of early

discussions between Robert and myself when discussing the Ori threat in this galaxy and how it would manifest itself," says executive producer Brad Wright, who penned the script.

Above: Samantha Carter (Amanda Tapping), Mitchell and Jackson confront the Prior.

Equally importantly, 'Beachhead' marked the re-appearance of *Stargate SG-1*'s leading lady, Amanda Tapping, who would be returning to set with her six-week old daughter Olivia. Her character, Samantha Carter, had been leading a Research and Development team at Area 51. Having already turned down a personal plea from Colonel Mitchell to rejoin SG-1 at the beginning of the year, the producers needed a really significant challenge that would require her expertise. "We had to have a big reason to bring her back, otherwise the reason for her being away would seem kind of lame," Robert Cooper points out.

Thankfully, they had just the thing hiding up their sleeves. "Rob was determined that the Ori should be from another galaxy," Wright explains, "so I thought it would require special means to travel that great a distance. The Supergate is an image that's been in the back of our minds for several seasons, but [we've been] saving for a special occasion."

"Brad's always wanted to do a big space gate," adds Cooper, with a laugh. "We did space gates in *Stargate: Atlantis*, and in fact, he wanted them to be Supergates [there] too, but that was just one step too many. We didn't need to go there, we didn't need to spend that cache just yet, we could save it — and I'm glad we did!"

Though finding the right story to re-integrate Sam Carter went very smoothly, actress Amanda Tapping admits that returning to the cast line-up so late in the year wasn't easy. There were new faces to get used to, both in front of and behind the camera. The huge revolution in the actress' own life, she says, coupled with these other changes at work, made for a peculiar and not altogether comfortable experience. "Personally, from my standpoint, I felt not a part of it," Tapping recalls. "The team had gelled, and I wasn't part of that process, [which] happens very early on in the season. I really had to break through and find my place on the team. I had a hard time at first, going, 'Do I still fit in on the show? Can I still hang with the guys? Here I am bringing my baby to work — is this still going to work?' It took a while."

Another task of the episode was to wave goodbye, at least temporarily, to Claudia Black and Vala Mal Doran. In doing so, the character managed to show yet another side of herself — this time as a self-sacrificing heroine.

"Claudia's original show deal was only for five episodes," Robert Cooper reveals. "Then, as the season started to progress, we realized that we really needed to give her a proper send-off and set up her potential return as well. It just didn't seem right to say goodbye to Vala and hello to Carter in the next episode. It needed a bit of a crossover, so we asked Claudia to do one more episode."

Carter: Reporting as ordered, sir.
Landry: [on phone] Yeah, she's standing right here. You're a funny man, Jack. Very funny.

Another particularly memorable aspect of 'Beachhead' was the guest star, Maury Chaykin, appearing as loathsome Goa'uld Nerus. Chaykin is another example of *Stargate SG-1*'s power to attract illustrious guest stars, and the actor's turn as Nerus proved one of the highpoints of the episode. "As far as Nerus is concerned, I thought that, considering most of the main Goa'ulds were gone, it might be fun to have a 'second tier' Goa'uld come to the forefront," says Wright. "I wrote the part with Maury Chaykin in mind, and was delighted when we were able to cast him."

Above: The Prior controls the wormhole.

The character of Nerus also enabled Beau Bridges to get his teeth into a rousing scene for Hank Landry, as the normally cool general finally loses his temper and in no uncertain terms puts the Goa'uld in his place. The actor has nothing but praise for his co-star of the moment. "Maury is just — wow!" Bridges says enthusiastically. "We had a lot of scenes together and I had never worked with him before [but] I'd heard about him. He's just so inventive. He's really a lot of fun, [and] such a bold performer. He just comes in, takes off all the limits and really goes for it."

Despite having to tie so many elements together in just one episode, the final cut of 'Beachhead' satisfied all of the demands placed upon it. Reporting himself to be pleased with the result, Brad Wright reveals that his original script had several aspects that had to be cut. "I didn't have to lose anything in editing," the executive producer explains, "but the first draft was quite long. There was a fun, albeit prohibitively expensive, attack upon the Supergate with F-302s that I had to lose for budgetary reasons anyway. In the end, I didn't have to leave anything on the editing room floor that I missed." Å

Ex Deus Machina

Written by: Joseph Mallozzi & Paul Mullie
Directed by: Martin Wood

Guest Cast: Simone Bailly (Ka'lel), Kevin Blatch (Tobias), Martin Christopher (Lieutenant Marks), Chilton Crane (Sheila Jameson), Kendall Cross (Julia Donovan), Ken Dresen (Alex Jameson), Peter Flemming (Agent Malcolm Barrett), Barclay Hope (Colonel Lionel Pendergast), David MacInnis (Agent Williams), Gardiner Millar (Yat'yir), Sonya Salomaa (Charlotte Mayfield), Cliff Simon (Ba'al)

The death on Earth of a Jaffa loyal to Gerak sends Mitchell and Teal'c to Dakara, while Daniel and Carter try to solve the mystery on Earth. Daniel's research throws up an aeronautics company whose financial officer has recently vanished. Gerak, meanwhile, is unwilling to answer questions. Unbeknownst to SGC, Gerak has the missing man, who is infected by a Goa'uld, as a prisoner. His employers on Earth refuse to answer questions about a works plant that recently closed but appears to be still operating, or what the missing man was working on when he disappeared. The company is actually home to the Goa'uld Ba'al, who is in hiding on Earth. Daniel suspects that the Goa'uld are still on Earth, gaining in strength, and both the Jaffa's death and the missing man are linked to a wider problem involving the Trust. Sure enough, Teal'c and Mitchell discover that Gerak sent his Jaffa to secure Ba'al. However, Teal'c has heard the former Goa'uld has recently been spotted elsewhere. SG-1 need to find Ba'al before Gerak can use him to gain power in the Jaffa council. Unfortunately, Gerak's torture of the missing man has led him straight to the Goa'uld's hiding place, and Gerak's Jaffa are now loose on Earth. Ba'al escapes, and then sends SGC a taped ultimatum: either his former enemies leave him alone, or he will detonate a naquadah bomb hidden somewhere in the USA. Confusion reigns when the NID and SGC try to arrest Ba'al — who appears to be in more than one place at once. Teal'c confronts Gerak about his activities on Earth while SGC prepares a missile loaded with symbiote poison. Carter realizes that a new building constructed in Seattle is full of naquadah, and Mitchell suggests the *Prometheus* beams it into deep space. Gerak kills one of the Ba'al clones, but more are still out there…

Landry: I'm not sure I understand, Colonel.
Sam: The bomb isn't in the building, sir. The bomb *is* the building.

Though battling the Ori and their religious machinations had taken center stage for season nine, the writers were still keen to provide a link to earlier seasons by revisiting past foes. 'Ex Deus Machina' did that by exploring the post-'Reckoning' fate of one old enemy, the Goa'uld Ba'al. The story also brought the attention of SGC — not to mention the attention of Earth's tentative allies, the Jaffa — very close to home.

Above: Former System Lord Ba'al (Cliff Simon) returns.

"We'd done six massive 'space opera, introduce the new bad guy' episodes," says Robert Cooper, "and the other thing we wanted to do in season nine was not completely abandon everything we'd done in the past. There was talk at the very beginning of, when you wipe the slate clean, you never quite get it all. There are always the rats that survive and crawl up from the sewers. So there was always an intention to have Goa'uld survive, and what would they be doing and how would they have carved out their little niches? And so 'Ex Deus Machina' is about Ba'al, and what happened to him after he escaped in 'Reckoning', and the fact that he is living on Earth."

Writer Joseph Mallozzi explains that his original idea was for a very different episode. "When I first pitched, it didn't take place on Earth," says Mallozzi. "It was essentially SG-1 and Teal'c's supporters in the High Council racing against Gerak and his supporters to locate Ba'al — they had discovered the location of one of his off-world strongholds. Teal'c and Gerak are vying for power, and they realize that whoever catches Ba'al first will win the hearts of many Jaffa. So they head off to Ba'al's stronghold, but what they don't realize is that Ba'al has set a trap for them. So they have to work together to escape. But after the first episodes, we really desperately needed a less expensive script. So Rob pitched out the possibility that it takes place on Earth."

Though the second pitch altered the writer's original intention for the episode, Mallozzi was happy with the eventual route that the story took. And the change opened the way for one of the most memorable teasers ever to introduce a *Stargate SG-1* story. "I wasn't exactly keen on the idea at first," admits Mallozzi, of the change of scene from off-world to Earth, "but we ended up spinning what I think is a terrific tease — this Jaffa running through the forest. You think, 'Oh, well, who is this Jaffa? What's going on?' and then the moment he's hit by the car, you realize 'Holy crap, he's on Earth!'"

Daniel: One [witness]. Some guy who was working overtime and spent most of the firefight under his desk, but was able to provide descriptions of three individuals: big, tattooed, chain-mail pants.

Mitchell: So it's either our Jaffa or Kiss is back on tour.

Unfortunately, even after the money-saving aspects of moving the action of the episode to Earth, 'Ex Deus Machina' continued to suffer from budgetary restrictions throughout production. For both writer Joseph Mallozzi and director Martin Wood, the episode eventually suffered for what the production couldn't afford to show.

"I liked it, don't get me wrong," clarifies Mallozzi, "but it's just one of those classic episodes where, unfortunately, we ended up telling more than showing. It would have been nice, for instance, to see the Jaffa attack on Ba'al's complex at the end, but it's just something that we couldn't do, so it had to happen off-screen."

"Ugh. A black mark, for me," says Wood candidly of the episode. "There are shows that you don't like that you did. 'Ex Deus Machina' was spread out over so much [shooting] time, and we had to pull so many integral elements out of it just to try and maintain the budget — it was just one of those shows that could have been better than it was. I could have done a better job than I did. It was just so pieced together over the course of six weeks that it just didn't feel good."

Given the time and budget, there are specific aspects of the episode that Wood would have liked to handle differently. "I would have shot it over an eight day period, rather than a six week period," he says, "that would have felt more cohesive to me. I would also have a couple of scenes that weren't in there. One is the clarification of, 'okay, we're firing this missile that's going to kill these Jaffa', then we've also got this whole thing about, 'we have to evacuate the building' happening. It felt like a big thing, evacuating the building, and a big thing killing all the Jaffa — and it was all off-screen. Whenever you have to do that, it's always a com-

Above: Teal'c (*Christopher Judge*) reflects on a disaster averted — and trouble ahead.

promise, no matter whether you're a writer or a director or the editor. If you have to do something like that off-screen, it's always a cheat and it always *feels* like that."

Despite the troubled aspects of producing it, Mallozzi maintains his appreciation of the episode. "I've always liked the Earth-centered episodes, and just the opportunity to have Ba'al settle into Earth society, I thought, was something not to be missed. It's interesting, because as Goa'uld they'll go from planet to planet and assume power and settle into whatever society they happen to have conquered. But in this case, obviously he's not going to be so overt about it, so rather than having him lord it over followers in his royal robes, he's in his three-piece suit and tie! And by the episode's end, you realize that Ba'al is not going to be that easy to get rid of. He's going to be around!" Å

Babylon

Written by: Damian Kindler
Directed by: Peter DeLuise

Guest Cast: William B. Davis (Prior), Bryan Elliot (Colonel Raimi), Jarvis George (Volnek), Jason George (Jolan), Darcy Laurie (Tass'an), Tony Todd (Lord Haikon)

SG-1 visit a world rumored to be home to the Sodan, Jaffa warriors who have not served the Goa'uld for 5,000 years. They are ambushed suddenly and, in the shoot-out, Mitchell injures a young Sodan. In response, the Sodan, who use an Ancient cloak to hide themselves from their enemies, take the injured Mitchell prisoner. SG-1 decide to take the young warrior back to SGC for treatment. Their search for Mitchell reveals only a stone gateway left by the Ancients, indicating that it is a path to enlightenment. On different planets, the two opposing warriors are treated for their wounds. Mitchell recovers enough to stand, and attempts to overcome his guard, Jolan, but fails. He is told that he must train for a fight to the death called the *kel shak lo* — he has spilled the blood of a Sodan warrior, and must atone for this sin. On Earth, the warrior, Volnek, is given Tretonin. Teal'c and Daniel try to convince him that the Sodan and Earth can be allies, but to no avail. Mitchell trains with Jolan, becoming fitter and fitter, but is told he is still not skilled enough to match the abilities of the Sodan he must fight. Gradually, though, Mitchell and Jolan form a mutual respect. When a Prior arrives through the gate, Mitchell realizes that this is why SG-1 were ambushed. The Ori claim to be the source of enlightenment the Sodan have craved for so long, and that Earth is the enemy. Mitchell tries to convince the Sodan leader, Lord Haikon, otherwise, but to no avail. Mitchell is slowly getting better, but still doesn't know who he is to fight. When the day finally arrives, Jolan is revealed to be his opponent — he is Volnek's brother. The fight commences, and Jolan betters Mitchell, apparently killing him. In fact, Jolan has only drugged him, and secretly lets him go, vowing to lead a resistance to the Prior's dominance over the Sodan. Back at the SGC, Mitchell confronts Volnek about the Ori before sending him home.

Volnek: You would never have survived *kel shak lo* alone.
Mitchell: Don't know. Took you down pretty good.

Having started season nine off at such a fast pace, the writers and producers had put aside giving the character of Cameron Mitchell his 'own'

Above: *Mitchell wonders about his dress sense.*

episode. By the time the slot of episode eight came around, however, it was felt it was high time to devote an entire story to SG-1's new leader, to get under his skin and see what made him tick. Even then, though, writer/producer Damian Kindler reveals that the idea for 'Babylon' wasn't even originally intended for *Stargate SG-1*.

"I had initially pitched a *Last Samurai*-type story as an *Atlantis* [episode], thinking it would be a great Teyla episode," he explains. "But Rob Cooper thought it would make a better Mitchell story, as his character had yet to be front-and-center in a *Stargate SG-1* story, what with all the Ori/Vala/Daniel business we were dealing with early on in season nine. So I knew from the get-go that this story was vital to revealing more about Cameron Mitchell than we'd seen up to that point. No pressure or anything, just make sure you do justice to the new lead of the series!"

Having opened up the idea of putting Mitchell in such a difficult position, Kindler reports that star Ben Browder was particularly happy with the story, and worked with the writer during the show's development. "I was very happy with how the script turned out, and so was Ben — who, whenever he could, stopped by my office to chat about the story. The main thing we talked about was how Mitchell's positive attitude manifests itself. We already knew about his near-death experience and determination to recuperate from his injuries. But it was fun to show how that works now when faced with overwhelming odds. He really doesn't ever give up, and that's what ultimately turns Jolan to his side — his unflinchingly positive attitude."

"'Babylon' was fun for me because I got to fall down a lot," laughs Browder. "I hadn't done anything very physical since 'Avalon, Part II', and I just love doing that sort of stuff for the few years I've got left to do it. So from a physical standpoint, it was a lot of fun. We were outside and running around... Any time we get to go outside and we're using weapons... It's a boy thing, I'm still a big ol' boy on the inside. I just love those days. There's [only] a select number of shows, or even films, where you get to do the action stuff. I relish that."

Jolan: May you die well.
Mitchell: Likewise.

Helming the episode was Peter DeLuise, veteran *Stargate SG-1* director, with plenty of experience in shooting scenes involving hand-to-hand combat. 'Babylon' was DeLuise's first experience of directing Browder, and to have such a physical episode to perfect so early on in their working relationship could have been difficult — but not so, according to the director. "Ben was a breath of fresh air, very enthusiastic, very physical," recalls DeLuise. "His enthusiasm, the things that he brought to the show and the amount of ideas that he had about what he wanted to do was really great. He was a real good team player, and he did a very large percentage of his own stunts, with the stick fighting on the sand — he threw himself down on the ground countless times."

DeLuise also added his own touches to Mitchell's training scenes, taking Damian Kindler's *Last Samurai* theme and the script's reflection of the Sodan's desire to keep their culture and extending it. "I was particularly happy with the community, the inclusion of the children," DeLuise explains. "There was a huge emphasis on preserving the Sodan culture. I also had the children watching the sparring, which was not in the script. For me, it helped us understand exactly how badly he was doing and how much he had improved, and how impressive his fighting ability was. Because you were watching the children react to

Above: *Mitchell learns to fight the Sodan way.*

those different criteria versus just watching it and making an assumption on your own. When you cut away to the kids, you can tell whether it's good or not. The kids [also] help us sell the idea that this was a culture worth preserving, that they were a unique society who deserve some sort of shot."

"I thought Peter DeLuise did a wonderful, wonderful job," enthuses Kindler. "No one understands the Jaffa like him. He knew exactly who the Sodan were right away, and really brought them to life. If anything, the episode suffered — ironically — from Ben's unquenchable enthusiasm. James ['Bam Bam'] Bamford, our stunt coordinator, put together an incredible sequence of fights, and worked them out with both Ben and his stunt double. But Ben insisted in doing virtually all his own fighting; wouldn't let his double do anything. Now the truth is, actors tend to be more tentative when fighting each other, but will really go for it when fighting a stunt person. So Ben did all his own fights, and as a result the fights ended up being slightly less vicious than Bam Bam envisioned. In his defense, Ben really worked his ass off on all fronts from the beginning to the end of 'Babylon'. Kudos to him." Å

Prototype

Written by: Alan McCullough
Directed by: Peter DeLuise

Guest Cast: Ivan Cermak (Major Altman), Neil Jackson (Khalek), Robert Picardo (Agent Richard Woolsey)

Sam leaves with SG-5 to investigate reports of another possible Ori incursion. However, the team is soon back — the planet they arrived on was not their intended destination. Running a diagnostic, it appears nothing is wrong at the SGC end — something must be redirecting anything organic before it reaches the destination gate. Finding a way to override it, SG-1 arrive on the planet and discover evidence of Goa'uld occupation in the form of transport rings that lead them to an underground laboratory. The lab houses a genetic manipulation device of the sort they have seen before, as well as a man in stasis. Mitchell accidentally revives him, and when he goes into shock, they take him to the SGC. He has been experimented on, though not by the Ancients, which was their first thought. Then Daniel makes a disturbing discovery: the laboratory belonged to Anubis, and the man, Khalek, was created by him. Khalek is a human-Goa'uld hybrid, made with Anubis' own DNA — essentially the Goa'uld's son. He is reaching the stage of Ascension rapidly, and they won't be able to control him. Daniel recommends that he be destroyed. However, Agent Woolsey arrives and demands that Khalek be studied, since the government believes he could provide an effective weapon against the Ori. They monitor his Ascension, which rapidly gets out of control — he escapes once, and is restrained. Sam and Daniel realize that the machine in the laboratory was treating Khalek gradually, and he requires a final treatment. Khalek breaks free, injuring Mitchell, and heads for the gateroom. He seems unstoppable, and activates the gate to escape. However, a few minutes later the wormhole returns Khalek to the SGC, where he is shot by Daniel and Mitchell. Carter used the gate-forwarding technology to trap him on Earth.

Mitchell: How can Woolsey not know that keeping this guy around is a bad idea?
Landry: He's an ass.

'Prototype' evolved from an idea first pitched by *Stargate SG-1*'s new staff writer, Alan McCullough, and as he explains, the story underwent a long evolution before it reached it's final incarnation. "I received the opportunity to pitch in January of 2005. I actually met with Rob Cooper in Toronto, at a book store," recalls the writer. "He was in town, and my agent had set up

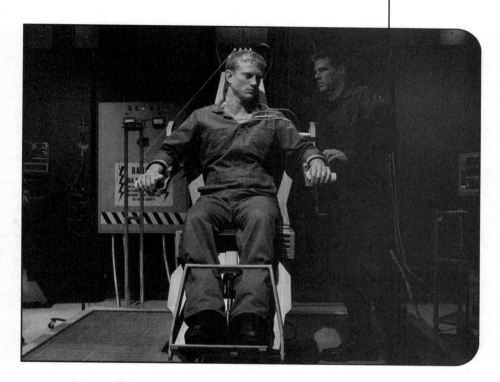

Above: Khalek (Neil Jackson), after revealing his true colors.

a meeting. We just talked in general about what they were looking for in season nine, and they liked one of my ideas enough to proceed. I wrote up an outline, and they flew me out [to Vancouver] and helped me shape it into what eventually became 'Prototype'. My first pitch resembled nothing of the final product. I think the door in was the same — they were trying to reach a certain planet and a device of some kind was re-routing them elsewhere. They had to break the code to get to that planet, but once there, they discover not Anubis' son in stasis, but some random master criminal whom the Goa'uld had locked there because they were afraid of him. But that was back when I had not as much familiarity with the show as I do now. That was part of the process, making it part of the *Stargate SG-1* mythology."

Getting the huge *Stargate SG-1* mythology right is daunting for any new writer, and is at the root of why the *SG-1* producers rarely take on new staff. Getting up to speed with the intricate history of each character over the past eight years requires hard work and a lot of trial and error, even for the most talented writer.

"It was a script that was very rich in the mythology," says McCullough, "it had to deal with the Ori, as well as Anubis and DNA manipulation. I wrote the first draft from Toronto, got notes, wrote a second draft, and I think by the time I hit the second draft, I had finally honed what they wanted. And they made me an offer as a result of that. Rob sent me something like fourteen hours of tapes from previous episodes, and then when I came out to Vancouver, they said, "You know what? You should also look at this, this and this…" and they sent me away with another six or seven! So by the end of it I think I had watched twenty or so hours to write the script."

Even having watched these episodes as background, the writer, formerly an actor, struggled to put the final draft together, particularly since this first script was written as a freelance project and McCullough was at home across the country in Toronto. "It was very difficult," he admits. "It was just a side that I'd never had. Writing when you're on staff, [if] you encounter a problem that you are not sure how to solve, you can just walk down the hall to where more experienced writers sit. But when you are at home and thousands of miles away — you hate to bother them on the phone with silly questions! It was a very difficult process. The voices — at the time there were some I'd never heard. Cameron Mitchell was a new character who had never appeared in *Stargate SG-1* before, so no matter how many past episodes I watched, I'd never seen Mitchell."

Sam: Oh, he's going to be okay. The Ascend-o-meter says Khalek is about eighty percent there.
Teal'c: 'Ascend-o-meter'?
Sam: Mitchell.

McCullough's perseverance paid off, however, and with a final polish from Robert Cooper, 'Prototype' made a fine addition to the *Stargate SG-1* cannon, and led the way to a new strand of mythology that would be explored more definitively the following year. It also gave the producers an opportunity to revisit a link from the 'old' show, which, amid the changes, provided continuity for loyal fans.

"That was another story that we had developed as a melding of the old and the new," Robert Cooper explains. "There are still remnants of all the storylines that we left behind, but how do they relate to the situation that we are in now? It was the story of Anubis' Frankenstein son, and how would we use that? How is everything we built in the past going to help us deal with it now? The Priors are essentially just advanced humans, people who have been artificially evolved by the Ori and given powers that we've seen other people in our galaxy have before. The Nirrti mutants [for example]. How was learning about this guy, who was on the cusp of Ascending and

also incredibly evil, going to help us down the line? So it became a stepping-stone into 'The Fourth Horseman'. But that episode was ultimately made by the actor who played Khalek, a British guy [named] Neil Jackson. He's just brilliant. He's on screen for so much time, and he's just riveting. He took the character and made him incredibly three-dimensional and scary."

'Prototype' also produced an opportunity for Michael Shanks to display an unexpected side of Daniel Jackson, as his understanding of the depth of Anubis' evil forced him to act. "It struck a different chord," Shanks explains. "It was a choice that had to be made that was very out of character for Daniel. Normally, his would be the voice protesting that we don't try and kill this guy, [but] he was the first one to say we *have* to kill this guy. So it was a very different beat to play for myself and for the character."

Shanks doesn't feel, however, that this display is an indication that Daniel has lost his trademark compassion. "I think that, as much as it could be deemed as turning a corner, it is very case-specific. That particular enemy caused a lot of grief and, for Daniel specifically, a lot of confrontation. So the idea that this is his legacy made it very easy for Daniel to make the choice that we have to get rid of this guy. At the end, that's exactly what happens. So I think that was significant to do." Å

Above: Agent Woolsey (Robert Picardo) darkens SG-1's door yet again.

The Fourth Horseman [Part 1]

Written by: Damian Kindler	Guest Cast: Tony Amendola (Bra'tac), Greg Anderson
Directed by: Andy Mikita	(Prior), Simone Bailly (Ka'lel), Cameron Bright (Orlin),
	Don S. Davis (General George Hammond), Jeff Judge
	(Aron), Gardiner Millar (Yat'yir), Ty Olsson (Colonel
	Barnes), Panou (Lieutenant Fisher), Julian Sands (Doci)

As Gerak's affiliation to the Ori is sealed, on Earth Carter and Dr Lee are working to create an anti-Prior device, developed from their experiences with Khalek. Colonel Barnes, recently returned from yet another Ori-converted planet, begins to develop symptoms of the Ori plague. Lieutenant Fisher of Barnes' team had no symptoms, and has left the base to attend a speech being given by Hammond. A quarantine order is issued, but it is not quick enough to stop the disease from taking hold on Earth. As Fisher is confirmed as a carrier, SGC's worst fears are realized. Teal'c, on Dakara, informs Landry that Gerak's preaching on behalf of the Ori is winning over the Jaffa. Teal'c and Bra'tac head for Chulak to speak with Jaffa who share their own anti-Ori thoughts, although this may provoke civil war. At Stargate Command, Carter is visited by a young boy who claims to be Orlin, her Ascended lover. He has returned to help solve Earth's crisis. His mind currently holds the wisdom of the Ancients, though it is fading fast as his mind degrades. He also brings information about the Ori. They use their worshipers to gain physical power, nothing more. While Sam and Orlin work on a cure, Dr Lee finishes the weapon — but still needs a sample of Prior blood to make it work. As Jackson, Mitchell and Carter go after a Prior, Teal'c and Bra'tac meet with Gerak, who does not want to kill his fellow Jaffa. The Prior behind his conversion is not impressed, and takes him to meet the Doci, where Gerak himself becomes a Prior. Mitchell and Jackson are captured by the Sodan, who are themselves considering whether to take the way of the Ori as their own. Earth is losing the battle against the plague, and Orlin still has no cure...

Dr Lee: You know, I keep telling myself that one of these days I'm going to do something that gets me a little respect.
Daniel: We're all waiting for that day, Bill.

Stargate SG-1's mid-season two-parters have become a lasting tradition, leaving viewers in North America on a cliff-hanging finale to help build excitement for the show's later return. Since season nine was going all-out to

Above: *Teal'c confronts a transformed Gerak (Louis Gossett Jr).*

make the year the biggest for the show to date, 'The Fourth Horseman' was always destined to be a huge episode. So huge, in fact, that a team of writers were called upon to pen what turned into a massive Earth-based epic.

"Rob [Cooper] had mentioned to me to think up ideas," recalls first-half writer Damian Kindler. "The first thing that came to me (thanks to 'The Powers That Be') was, what if a Prior plague came to Earth? But I immediately thought, how the hell could we do that? It'd be too big. So I told Rob about it and said, 'So really, it's about another planet being hit by the plague and it might get to Earth.' He said, 'No, infect Earth right away. We can do it like *Outbreak*.' He also wanted to explore how the Priors were influencing the shifting political tides amongst the Jaffa. So I got the nod to pen part one, while Joe Mallozzi and Paul Mullie would write part two."

Though they would essentially be writing two different episodes, in an attempt to make the task a little easier on themselves, the writers worked together right from the start to produce a solid outline for the piece. "Writing two-parters is challenging enough as it is," laughs Mallozzi, "but writing the second half when someone else is writing the first part is *extremely* challenging! So Damian and I got together and we went back and forth."

"Paul [Mullie] was busy for a time producing *Stargate: Atlantis*," Kindler goes on to explain, "so Joe and I spent a lot of time breaking both parts of 'The Fourth Horseman' on the board, and spinning ideas around. I wrote a few drafts of my script, but to his credit, he really contributed a huge amount to both parts. He's tireless and passionate about the show."

There was one major disappointment for all concerned when it was discovered that one of their planned guest stars would not be available. Sean Patrick Flannery, who had appeared in season five's 'Ascension', would not be able to reprise his role as the Ascended being Orlin, whose love for Sam Carter had caused him to temporarily take human form. With this came a new, sticky task — rewriting the scripts to cover Flannery's absence.

Landry: According to the mission report, on your first encounter with Orlin, you two had an... intimate relationship?
Sam: Uh, well, we did. But, uh, he didn't look like that. He was...
Lam: Taller?

"I'm not sure at what point [we found out] Sean Patrick Flannery was not going to be available," says Mallozzi. "We tried, but it just didn't work with his schedule. So there was much discussion, and people pointed out, 'Well, if he descends, it doesn't matter what he looks like.' But it just seemed odd. If he could come back as the same person, the same physical appearance, why wouldn't he? The fact that he didn't have to is not a good enough excuse. And then Brad [Wright] had the image of him coming back as a young boy. And I thought, 'Well, that's interesting, but why would he come back as a young boy?' Then I remembered, [from] way back when I was taking psychology, reading that children's brains are hot-wired differently than adult brains and that sometime around adolescence, their brain kind of switches. And I thought, well, maybe that's something interesting that I can take advantage of. So, the reason that he comes back as a young boy is his brain is different than an adult's, he's able to retain more memory, able to learn a lot faster. He knows that his memories will eventually fade, but he chooses to come back as a young boy because he'll be able to retain more of his memories. So that's how we answered that."

In turn, the casting of a child actor in the role of Orlin caused its own problems, particularly for director Andy Mikita. Chosen for the part was

Canadian performer Cameron Bright. At the time, Bright had recently caused a stir by starring opposite Nicole Kidman in controversial movie *Birth*.

"He's a local actor out of Victoria, so he was accessible to us," Mikita explains. "Boy, talk about a shed full of work! He had massive passages of dialogue to commit to memory, and it required a lot of work from him. He had so much to do in the episode, and that was actually probably the single biggest concern for me when I read the script, hiring a kid for these huge scenes. He's a pivotal character for the show. And to his credit he did a terrific job. There was one day where we were shooting a scene in the briefing room that had to have been five pages long, and he had the lion's share of the dialogue. He came in, sat down, and when we did our

Above: Daniel Jackson finds himself in a tight spot.

first rehearsal, he didn't even need a script. He knew *everything*. He had all his dialogue down. And that's more than can be said for a lot of grown up actors! That was really fortunate. That was one of the things that could have killed us, not just from a production standpoint. It could have either made or broken the show, and he just did so well that it really helped make it."

Actress Amanda Tapping also has nothing but praise for her young co-star, who she spent a lot of time with, both on- and off-camera, during the episode's shoot. "'The Fourth Horseman' definitely stands out to me," she says. "It's a weird dynamic to play, because he has all the memories of this sexual being, this adult, but he's a little kid. So it's kind of freaky. But it was neat to play off [Cameron], he has a really interesting stillness to him. He was a really cool kid, he talked about 'kid' things — we talked a lot about paintball and skateboards! He hung out in the trailer with me and Olivia. [He has] a lot of experience, but was still a kid, which was great. I was nervous that he might be one of those child actors who is too self-assured and very pompous, in a way. But there's nothing pompous about Cameron, he's really sweet." Å

Written by: Joseph Mallozzi & Paul Mulllie

Directed by: Andy Mikita

Guest Cast: Tony Amendola (Bra'tac), Simone Bailly (Ka'lel), Cameron Bright (Orlin), Gary Chalk (Colonel Chekov), Noah Danby (Cha'ra), William B. Davis (Prior), Don S. Davis (General George Hammond), Kurt Evans (Colonel Johnson), Jason George (Jolan), Jeff Judge (Aron), Mark Oliver (LaPierre), Tony Todd (Lord Haikon)

Teal'c and Gerak, in his Prior state, argue about whether the Jaffa should follow the Ori. On Earth, the disease is spreading beyond US borders, and a sick Orlin still has no cure. Carter tries to convince him to simply write down the information she needs, but he refuses even though he is suffering permanent brain damage. Lord Haikon of the Sodan has become convinced that the Ori are false gods, and asks for Mitchell's help. Daniel and Mitchell have a device that will disrupt the Prior's ability to communicate with their masters and restrict their powers, but it's untested. Mitchell plans to test it himself, then, providing it works, they will take a blood sample for SGC and convince the Prior to turn against the Ori. Gerak is winning, and Teal'c and Bra'tac retreat to Chulak to gather support and form an uprising to force Gerak's hand. On Earth, Orlin is forced to give up his pursuit of the cure as news arrives that it has gone global — and even Landry is infected. Mitchell and Daniel manage to trap a Prior but make little headway in convincing him of the Ori's malevolence. Teal'c's last-ditch attempt to stop Gerak from turning the Jaffa over to a new slavery for the Ori works, but Gerak knows that he will not survive his decision. He uses his Prior-given powers to cure everyone infected at the SGC, bursting into flames as they are healed. Their purged blood provides the cure for the rest of the world fortunate enough to be alive — but 3,000 are dead. Orlin lives, but is merely a child now — no remnants of his Ancient history remain.

Daniel: Why did they send you to this galaxy in the first place?
Prior: We are beacons on the road to enlightenment.

Having already been forced to juggle guest characters to make the first half of 'The Fourth Horseman' work, Joseph Mallozzi then found that circumstances prevailed upon him to do the same for part two. "Originally, Michael [Shanks] was not going to be available for the episode," the executive

producer explains. "He was going to be available, but he was going to have to be very light. Then it turned out that he was not going to be light, so we put him back in and found a way to give him a more active role in the episode. Then General Jumper, the Air Force Chief of Staff, was supposed to make a cameo. I had written a couple of scenes [for him] with Landry, but it turned out that he was not going to be available, so we re-wrote the episode for General Hammond, and it also included a scene at the very end. In the original script, the scene didn't exist, but I wrote it for Don [S. Davis], and specifically for General Hammond. He comes into the office, and he's briefly re-united with the new SG-1 minus, unfortunately, Teal'c. We weren't able to get the character into the room, just because of the way the script was written. But I thought it was important that if Hammond came back, he had a moment with his old team."

For Mallozzi, the very element that had made Damian Kindler originally shy away from setting 'The Fourth Horseman' on Earth — not being able to adequately display the scale of the disaster — ultimately did affect the success of the episode. "It's a fine episode, but to be honest it's not my favorite this season. It's another episode where we're unfortunately telling more than we were showing, just because the magnitude of a plague ravaging the planet is very hard to convey visually on a TV show. You've got a lot of news reports, and hopefully it worked up to a certain point, but I think that the episode may have suffered slightly because of that."

"We still had some good sequences," director Andy Mikita points out. "The little action sequence of the Prior throwing Mitchell around, that was a lot of fun. We were down on the village set, and we had Ben on a high-wire rig. We were talking about a number of different ways of dealing with it in pre-production — what should we have the Prior do? Should we have him pick Mitchell up and throw him against the building, or should we just pull him up? We worked on that in advance, and there was going to be certain issues with the amount of time that we had to shoot the scenes. So part of that gag was just the result of production limitations. What could we actually get away with, time- and money-wise, that would still be a fun thing to do?"

Teal'c: Why do you hesitate, Gerak?
Gerak: If I help you, I will die. But I will die free!

Though the production could have had a stunt performer fill in for Browder during the wire-work scenes, the actor chose to get into the harness himself. "The actual physical wire work itself was worked out between the special effects guys and Ben, and what he was comfortable doing," Mikita continues. "At first, I wanted to have Ben literally just hoisted up to about fifteen or twenty feet off the ground, just a straight pull up. [But] because of the harness, the momentum caused Ben to do a bit of a somersault. He and I had a fair amount of conversation about it when we were filming. I thought it was going to be more fun if he was just hoisted straight up, and Ben thought it might be more fun if he actually did a bit more of a loose spin. So we discussed that a fair bit on the set at the time, and it worked out great. So much of it ends up getting adjusted on the day, when you're actually filming. We, unfortunately, didn't have the opportunity to do too much testing, we had to just bring the big crane up to the set, and when it came time to shoot those scenes say, 'Okay! Let's hope the plan works!' And I think it did work pretty well."

Another cause for anxiety for the director was an element of the script that had carried over from the final scenes of 'The Fourth Horseman, Part I'. With the revelation that Jaffa leader Gerak had 'gone to the dark side' and embraced the Ori came a particularly demanding sequence of filming for Oscar-winning guest star Lou Gossett.

"It was great having Lou Gossett," says Mikita. "Getting him into the make-up was a big deal. That was a big amount of work for Lou to do. Putting a seasoned actor like him into prosthetic make-up and giving him big long passages of dialogue is pretty tough. We had to make a few adjustments to the make-up. The first application we did on him, he was wearing these big cumbersome costumes, which look spectacular but are uncomfortable. The make-up was causing him to perspire to the point where the [prosthetic] was literally falling off. It was very uncomfortable for him, particularly given the fact that he had to sit for four hours before call time to have the make-up put on. That's not something you like to do to a seventy-plus year-old man, especially an Academy Award-winning actor of his stature. So there were all those

Above: General Hammond (Don S. Davis) returns!

concerns, and we definitely had to make adjustments. He and I worked through the scenes ahead of time as much as we could, just to make sure that it was going to be comfortable for him. But he was always reasonable — he's a seasoned pro, he knows what it takes. He didn't at any time try to make anything difficult for anybody. We gave him quite a work out, but he's such a team player."

"Two things really stood out for me in the episode," concludes Mallozzi, "Chris [Judge]'s performance, especially in that scene where he convinces Gerak to turn, and the Lam/Landry exchange, where Landry is lying on what could be his death bed, and they have a conversation about the past and her mother. I thought that was brilliant. It's just one scene, but Beau lent it such gravity. It's one of those instances where the scene as shot is better than the script as written. Believe me," he laughs, "that doesn't happen often!" Λ

Collateral Damage

Written by: Joseph Mallozzi & Paul Mullie Directed by: William Waring	Guest Cast: William Atherton (Emissary Varta), Anna Galvin (Dr Reya Varrick), Warren Kimmel (Dr Marell), Ian Robison (Mitchell's Father), Benson Simmonds (Dr Amuro), John Treleaven (Colonel Davidson), Maximillian Uhrin (Young Mitchell)

Mitchell dreams of beating a woman to death. He wakes to find himself in a strange house with blood on his hands and is arrested for the murder of Dr Reya Varrick. SG-1 have been visiting Galar, a world whose experiments with memory implantation adapted from a Goa'uld memory device have been very successful. The educational potential is amazing, and Earth is eager to trade with the Galarans if possible. To seal their new friendship, SG-1 attended a party on Galar. An outburst ensued when Dr Varrick learned the Galaran emissary had moved forward military tests, which she vehemently opposed. When she left, Mitchell followed. She explained that the military want the technology. Sharing a kiss with the scientist is the last thing Mitchell remembers clearly before being arrested. When he tells his team he can remember killing Reya and feeling a burst of insane anger, Daniel is convinced it's a memory implant, but Mitchell doesn't know what to believe. The Galaran government don't want to jeopardize trade relations with Earth and release him. They even offer to remove the memory. Mitchell refuses — he wants to know what really happened, whatever the consequences. Dr Varrick's colleagues, including a Dr Marell, believe the military killed her, and try to help Mitchell clear his name. They run tests to see if his memories have been altered. Daniel and Teal'c, meanwhile, find that Dr Varrick's personal records have been deleted. Unfortunately for Mitchell, Dr Marell can't find evidence that he didn't kill Dr Varrick. To complicate matters, Marell reveals that Reya was his ex-wife and he wants no more to do with Mitchell's case. Mitchell persuades Marell to try again, and this time they find evidence that he isn't guilty; an anomaly that indicates a memory splice. The killer is actually Marell. He implanted Mitchell and then erased his own memories. Mitchell's mind is restored, but the emissary wipes Marell's memories — so that he can continue working on the project.

Landry: I read your report. Not sure I've ever seen language like that used in an official Air Force document before.
Mitchell: Sorry about that, sir.

Above: *Mitchell discovers new attractions to space travel.*

Arguably the most controversial episode of *Stargate SG-1* to date, 'Collateral Damage' showed a level of violence that had never before been seen in the series. Whereas previously the show had shied away from being too explicit in its handling of brutality, for this episode executive producer Robert Cooper deliberately wanted to push the envelope of what had previously been acceptable for the show. "I went to the director and told him to just totally take the reigns off," Cooper recalls. "It's very violent, and it's very dark. I said to Will [Waring], 'I want to see shots of Mitchell killing this person. That's what this is about.' It's portraying what he's going through in having this memory, and how horrible it is for him to have to carry this. Watching it, and looking at the way it's cut and the way it's shot — there's your hero bludgeoning this woman to death. It's pretty disturbing.

"The network, I think, invites that sort of controversy, because it draws attention to the show and that's good. Obviously, they don't want people to turn the show off, and I think they were concerned about that with 'Avalon'. On the other hand, it is good television. 'Collateral Damage' is told in a responsible way, and it's a quality dramatic moment. It's not gratuitous, it's not something that doesn't serve the story. It's just a hell of a lot darker than anyone's ever seen before on *Stargate SG-1*. And it's not us trying to be more like anybody else — we're still *Stargate SG-1*, but we are pushing the limits and boundaries a little more. Paul [Mullie] did a brilliant job writing it, and

Will Waring did a brilliant job directing it. It's a great little sci-fi twist of Mitchell having a memory implant. But the real reason for doing the story is the opportunity to explore Mitchell's past."

"It is a very, very dark episode," agrees Joe Mallozzi, "and I think it is probably one of the best episodes of season nine. This one was interesting, [because] it's actually a pitch I pitched out two years ago. Then it was Teal'c who goes to a planet, has his memories implanted and he's charged with a murder. But we pitched it back and forth, and that became season eight's 'Affinity', which was completely different. So I pitched it again and it became Mitchell. I wrote the outline, but I was working on 'Ripple Effect' at that point, so Paul wrote the script and did, I thought, a terrific job. It was a great opportunity to get some insight into Mitchell's background and character, which is something that we didn't really get a chance to do in the first half of the season, because we were dealing with the Ori and we had so many 'housekeeping' issues to deal with. But it's great. It's an incredibly dark episode, especially the tease where we actually see Mitchell, our hero, bludgeon a woman to death."

Jackson: It wasn't you, okay? These people can implant memories.

Mitchell: Yeah, I've been trying to tell myself the same thing all morning. It doesn't stop me from still seeing her face.

The episode also gave the crew the opportunity to try something technically different, very appropriate considering the mold-breaking material of the story itself. "It was out of the realm of what we [normally] do, it's quite a bit darker. With a story like that, where you're going into memories, it's eye candy," says the director, Will Waring, with a laugh. "Open the drawer and let's have some fun!"

That sense of "fun" came partly from the flashback sequences, which gave Waring and *Stargate SG-1*'s long-standing director of photography, Peter Woeste, a chance to really put something different on screen. In particular, they wanted to produce a different tone, not only to indicate to the viewers when the story was in flashback mode, but also to enhance the natural tension of the script. Surprisingly, the answer came from something distinctly low-tech, an anachronism in today's technologically advanced film industry.

"We were bouncing around a lot of ideas of what we could do for the flashback sequences," Waring explains. "Peter Woeste said, 'Hey, I've got this Bolex in my basement.' A Bolex is a 1950s home movie camera. It's about

Above: *Carter helps Mitchell clear his mind.*

the size of a good novel, with a wind-up handle on the side. You could spring wind it and press a button and it would shoot. But you could also set it to hand crank the camera. Film is supposed to run at twenty-four frames a second, which gives the movement that you see on [modern] screens. But when you hand crank it, you're not really sure what you're getting. You kind of gauge by the sound of the machine — 'That sounds like twenty-four, or maybe it's twenty, maybe it's six. We'll just change it around a bit.' We did some tests, and it was such crazy fun to watch that we just went with that. So all of the flashbacks of the murder were shot with that, and *only* with that. So here's Pete, who's six-foot-five, with this little camera that barely fits in his hand," laughs the director, "and he was doing all the hand cranking. The subject matter of what we were filming was horrific, but the way we were doing it was just so incongruous, it was very, very funny."

Using this tiny mechanical camera gave Waring and Woeste exactly the effect they were looking for, and in post-production they were able to put the finishing touches on one of *Stargate SG-1's* most memorable episodes. "We played with it in editing, and that's what gave the different speed changes. The light would change, because as Pete slowed down [the hand cranking] it would over-expose the film and 'blow out'," Waring says, describing the light flare and color difference seen in the flashback sequences. "We could cut that up a bit and make it faster, or make it blow out more. I think it worked really quite well." Å

Ripple Effect

Story by: Brad Wright and Joseph Mallozzi & Paul Mullie
Teleplay by: Joseph Mallozzi & Paul Mullie
Directed by: Peter DeLuise

Guest Cast: JR Bourne (Martouf), Morris Chapdelaine (voice of Kvasir), Teryl Rothery (Janet Fraiser), Dan Shea (Sergeant Siler)

SG-1 (wearing black uniforms) return from an off-world mission earlier than expected, preceded by a strange power surge in the gate. They don't seem to be affected by the surge, and the debrief continues — they've been to a village that has been visited by the Ori. Suddenly, the gate activates again, at the time SG-1 were actually scheduled to return, and another identical team appears (though wearing green uniforms). The Carters believe an intersection of parallel universes could be to blame. The question is, how did the black-uniformed team get to 'our' universe and how does SGC return them to their own reality? The Carters discuss the problem, and realize that the wormhole they took to get to Earth bisected a black hole. They continue to work as more and more teams arrive — including some old friends in the form of Dr Janet Fraiser and Martouf. The black-uniformed Carter believes that the intersection originated in her universe, and that it can be closed if they detonate a huge charge at the exact point where an open wormhole meets the quantum singularity — though doing so will mean that the multiple teams are trapped in this universe. The SGC contact the Asgard and borrow a time-dilation device to help them position the charge. SG-1 boards the *Prometheus* alongside their black-uniformed doppelgängers. Unbeknownst to our SG-1, the other SG team deliberately caused the convergence of universes in order to sabotage the subsequent mission and steal the *Prometheus*. They intend to use the *Prometheus* to steal the ZPM from our Atlantis and return to their own reality, then use the ZPM to power their Ancient weapon and stop their Ori. SG-1 outsmart the other team, and Carter realizes that now they know how the convergence was created, she can recreate those conditions and send all their counterparts back. It involves firing a high-energy weapon at the gate, but it works. The teams depart, and despite the actions of the errant SG-1, SGC lets them go to find another way to fight the Ori in their own universe.

Teal'c: You were honored with a hero's funeral.
Fraiser: Lucky me.

'Ripple Effect', though essentially a concept that *Stargate SG-1* had visited many times before, proved to be one of the most complicated episodes of the season — and one of the most loved by fans. Quite unexpectedly, the episode also returned two favorite recurring characters to our screens from the show's past, in the shape of JR Bourne as the Tok'ra Martouf and Teryl Rothery as Stargate Command's own beloved Dr Janet Fraiser.

For Rothery, returning to the show that she had left in a hail of staff-weapon fire more than two years previously was particularly surreal because of the significant cast changes for season nine. Gone were George

Above: Dr Janet Fraiser (Teryl Rothery), alive and well.

Hammond and Jack O'Neill. Instead, in their place were faces the character hadn't experienced before — whatever parallel universe she inhabited. As a result, the Janet that appeared through the wormhole was very different to the mild-mannered physician viewers remember, particularly in her dealings with General Hank Landry. "I made the decision that I didn't know who this person was, and there was not a lot of love lost there," the actress intimates. "When you first see her with him, there are some looks towards him like, 'Who is this person?' She's still taking in the fact that he's wearing his General's epaulettes, but it's definitely different. There's a slight warming up at the end when I leave. It would make sense — she spent years working with General Hammond. Hammond brought her into the program."

Besides the emotional side of the episode, the production also had to battle with the massive logistics of producing an episode with so many multiples of its main characters. "It was a huge episode to shoot," says Amanda Tapping, "Peter DeLuise did a great job. I think at one point there were fifteen of me in the scene! We shot them all individually with a stop-motion camera, and it was insane. It took us eight-and-a-half hours to shoot that one scene. In my recollection, never has a scene that was seemingly short on the page (that wasn't full of mortars and people flying through the air) taken that long to shoot," she laughs. "There were no stunts, it was just a huge visual effects episode!" Å

(See page 100 for an in-depth look at the making of this episode.)

Stronghold

Written by: Alan McCullough **Directed by:** Peter DeLuise	**Guest Cast:** Tony Amendola (Bra'tac), Simone Bailly (Ka'lel), Eric Breker (SG-3 Leader), Reed Diamond (Major Bryce Ferguson), Yan Feldman (Til'vak), Dakin Matthews (Maz'rai), Gardiner Millar (Yat'yir), Cliff Simon (Ba'al), Veena Sood (Dr Kelly), Don Thompson (U'kin)

Teal'c and Bra'tac attend a meeting of the Jaffa High Council in which they fully expect a movement towards democracy for the new Jaffa Nation to be ratified. Instead, their supporter suddenly changes tack. Meanwhile, on Earth, Mitchell is taking some personal time to visit Major Bryce Ferguson, an old friend and comrade suffering from a terminal condition — shrapnel embedded in his brain, an injury suffered during a brave act to save Mitchell's own life. His friend wants to know what Mitchell is working on now, but of course the colonel can't tell him. At Stargate Command, Bra'tac arrives to inform Landry and the team that Teal'c has disappeared. Sam and Daniel go to Dakara to help with the search, while Mitchell remains with Ferguson. Bra'tac concludes that his allies in the council, including Maz'rai, have been brainwashed, but by whom he cannot tell. Teal'c, meanwhile, is at the mercy of a Ba'al clone, undergoing torture designed to make him Ba'al's loyal servant. Having been confronted by Daniel and Bra'tac, Maz'rai attempts to perform an ancient Jaffa rite on himself, but is later found dead, having written down the name of another council member. Once they think they have found where Teal'c is being held, Landry arranges an attack force, led by Mitchell, who leaves Ferguson to experience the adventures of his last few months via the Galaran memory device. Bra'tac is shot and injured during the attack, and brought before Ba'al, who orders Teal'c — who has apparently succumbed to the brainwashing — to kill his friend and mentor. Teal'c is actually faking it, and when Mitchell arrives to help, they and Bra'tac overcome Ba'al and his soldiers. Arriving back home, Mitchell discovers that in saving the life of one friend, he has missed the last hours of another — Ferguson has passed away.

Landry: Teal'c is family. I don't like people screwing with my family.

'Stronghold' was the second episode penned by newcomer Alan McCullough, who had been taken on as permanent staff following his successful previous episode 'Prototype'. This episode would focus heavily on

Above: *Teal'c suffers for his people.*

two characters, both for the most part following separate plot lines — Teal'c and Cameron Mitchell. For McCullough, writing 'Stronghold' would mean tackling the voice he had previously found most difficult to get right, that of the Jaffa Teal'c.

"It's funny, because at the time that I wrote 'Prototype', I didn't think I'd had a problem in writing Teal'c," says the writer with a laugh. "I was told after I arrived [on staff] that Teal'c's voice was the one they found least accurate. [But] once I hit the ground in Vancouver, I started reading scripts, and the way I'm wired, I can hear the voices off the page almost better than I can hear them on the screen. So I found when I started reading a lot of Teal'c's voice after arriving, I was able to get him a little better. Obviously Rob Cooper or Brad Wright always do a pass after the second draft, and I certainly didn't nail Teal'c's voice in 'Stronghold', but I got a lot closer, I think. How did I deal with Teal'c's voice? I think it's less robotic. That's the note I got most on 'Prototype': 'He's not a robot. He's stoic and he speaks in succinct phrases, but they're not devoid of emotion.'"

Some of the most challenging scenes of 'Stronghold' involved Teal'c's torture at the hands of Ba'al, who actually wasn't in McCullough's original pitch. "When I came in, I pitched a story where Teal'c was kidnapped," the writer explains. "I didn't involve Ba'al at the time, that was something that was brought in as a result of us meeting to break the story."

In fact, the inclusion of Teal'c's torture caused some problems for one of the show's stars, namely Christopher Judge, who was concerned that putting the stoic character in such a position could make him appear weak. "That's something that I initially fought against," says Judge. "But in retrospect I think it was the right choice, because they showed some evidence of the amount of torture he was going through. If I had been silent it could have left a question — how much is he going through? But we see that this has actually gone beyond his threshold of pain."

Ba'al: I'm curious. Are you merely feigning allegiance, waiting for the right time to strike at me?

Another large part of 'Stronghold' is the strand of the story that finds Mitchell struggling to come to terms with the impending death of his friend, Bryce Ferguson. For executive producer Robert Cooper, this was a unique way to further explore the personality of their new leading character. "There was the ultimate situation of Teal'c getting in trouble and [SG-1] having to go save him," explains Cooper, "and Mitchell was potentially going to be held back from that. That produces a great amount of dramatic tension — the audience is going to be saying, 'God, I want Mitchell to go and save the day,' and yet he's got this other thing he's got to do out of an emotional responsibility. It gives us an opportunity to play a little bit with who he is, and let us get to know him a little better. The dying friend story has been done a million times, and I think we came up with a different twist on it, which was interesting to try. It's not about 'My friend is dying and I've got to do something for him' — it's the dying friend trying to do something for Mitchell, which is kind of releasing him from his burden."

This approach was in fact so different that director Peter DeLuise was himself not expecting it. Instead of what he terms the 'traditional' pay-off that would usually come into play in such a set-up, the director had to find another way of bringing the story to a satisfactory conclusion in his own mind. "I thought for sure that Mitchell was going to invite him through the Stargate," recalls DeLuise, "and his friend was going to get to see the cool outerspace job that Mitchell has, and sacrifice his life in the line of duty in some special way — like by blowing up all the bad guys because he was terminally ill anyway — or get a Goa'uld or something to fix him. So when that didn't happen, I was quite surprised! I didn't understand how this was supposed to pay off the story. When I asked Robert about it, he said, 'Well, I want to get some backstory to Mitchell, and I want him to understand about

Above: Ba'al examines his captive.

duty and laying down your life and doing the right thing.' So what he was doing was having this emotional journey for Mitchell to show how he deals with his own demons, and also why he was so gung-ho to help save Teal'c — because somebody had risked their own life for him."

For the scenes in which Mitchell conversed with Ferguson at his bedside, DeLuise had a specific style he wanted to impose as director. "I wanted them to overlap their dialogue and to ad lib appropriately, so it had that realistic feel to it," he explains. "It was more accessible [that way]. I wanted them to feel like real people that you recognized. We brought the PlayStation in there, and they were playing games. I wanted them to feel like all-American guys that had just had this bad thing happen to them, but that didn't change the fact that they were good guys."

The other memorable aspect of 'Stronghold' was the battle scene in which Teal'c is rescued. "That was quite daunting," recalls the director, "because we didn't even have a whole day to do the firefight, just a partial day. I thought, for the amount of time we spent on it, that it came out really well. Normally, when you do a sequence that big, you take a few days. But we just ended up spending about ten hours on that sequence. The bombs and the fire, that can slow everything down, but our guys are really, really good. It worked out!" Å

Ethon

Story by: Damian Kindler and Robert C. Cooper
Teleplay by: Damian Kindler
Directed by: Ken Girotti

Guest Cast: John Aylward (President Nadal), Matthew Bennett (Jared Kane), Martin Christopher (Captain Marks), Barclay Hope (Colonel Lionel Pendergast), Chelah Horsdal (Lieutenant Womack), Ernie Hudson (Pernaux), Desiree Zurowski (Minister Chaska)

Jared Kane of the Rand Protectorate on the planet Tegalus arrives at Stargate Command asking for SG-1's help, without authorization from his government. The Protectorate have been visited by a Prior, who gave them plans for an orbital weapons platform capable of destroying their enemies, the Caledonians. Kane wants Earth's help to stop his government using the weapon — he doesn't want the Ori to dictate policy. Mitchell wants to destroy the weapon, but Daniel thinks they should try to convince the Rand government of the Ori threat. Carter examines the weapon's blueprints Kane brought, and believes that though it could wield massive power, it isn't active yet. The Protectorate agrees to meet with Daniel, but when he and Kane gate to Tegalus, they are arrested for treason. The *Prometheus*, carrying Teal'c, Carter and Mitchell, approaches the planet. The ship prepares to destroy the satellite, but it powers up — clearly fully functional after all. Mitchell and Teal'c launch in an F-302, but Earth's battleship is destroyed and only some of her crew and Carter manage to evacuate. Daniel continues to try and convince the Rand government about the Ori, and eventually one, Pernaux, seems sympathetic. President Nadal, however, prepares to fire the weapon at Caledonia. Having managed to reach the Caledonian government, Carter suggests firing an EM pulse missile at the Rand Protectorate to knock out their ability to control the weapon, allowing Mitchell and Teal'c to destroy it before it can fire. The pulse works, and Nadal agrees to discuss a diplomatic solution, so Mitchell calls off his strike on the weapon. But Nadal was merely stalling for time, and suddenly launches an attack. Pernaux kills him, promising to initiate peace talks with the other side. However, days later the talks break down. When Earth can't contact either side it is presumed that they have wiped each other out.

Kane: Do you ever give up?
Daniel: Not until I'm dead. And sometimes not even then...

Opposite: Samantha Carter, still the same genius at work.

'Ethon' revisited the troubled world of Tegalus, a planet divided by bitter and bloody conflict, originally made all the worse by SG-1's visit in

season eight's episode 'Icon'. Executive producer Robert Cooper co-wrote the story outline with Damian Kindler, writer of the earlier episode. "Rob wanted to go back there," Kindler explains. "I always feel lame pitching stories set on worlds I created previously, like you're mining your own seam too deep — 'Hey, how 'bout another Felger screw-up story?' But Rob walked into the office and just had the idea in his head. So we discussed it and seeing I had done 'Icon', I got to develop the idea further into a story."

Cooper reveals that, actually, the idea for 'Ethon' (the name of the mythological eagle that gnawed at the liver of the Titan Prometheus) primarily arose out of a difficult practical problem on set rather than a desire to revisit Tegalus itself. "That one came from a set," Cooper continues. "We had one set that was swinging between the *Prometheus* and the *Daedalus* [on *Stargate: Atlantis*], and every time we went back and forth between them we would have to change them over. Of course, the *Daedalus* was a really cool looking ship, and we were looking at the *Prometheus* going, '*Stargate SG-1*'s ship is not as cool as *Stargate: Atlantis*' ship — that's not fair!'"

Mitchell: Maybe one of us will get lucky and take a portion of the next shot.
Teal'c: I would not consider that lucky, Colonel Mitchell.
Mitchell: Well it could be for anybody aboard *Prometheus*.

Since the *Prometheus* had served the show so very well, the producers were loath to simply retire the ship without a fanfare. Writing it out instead gave the writers an opportunity to do something that could really take advantage of the VFX department's talents, inspired by the death of another famous vessel. "We thought, 'We've got to have it go out in a blaze of glory,'" recalls Cooper, "and I said, 'Let's do '*Titanic* in space' with the *Prometheus*!' That's always what it was meant to be — that scene where you see the *Titanic* go down. For once, we didn't win. We didn't go in and solve every problem, and we got burnt for it. We go in, mess up, and a massive, massive tragedy happens. Every once in a while you have to lose some people, and deal with that reality."

Visual effects are a huge component of both *Stargate SG-1* and *Stargate: Atlantis*, and this time, the team would have their work on screen for a protracted length of time, at the specific request of the executive producer. "The visual effects on this show always tend to be very quick. I talked to them all about this sequence when we were spotting," says Cooper, speaking of the process in which the team sits down and works out

Above: *Jackson tries to find a peaceful solution.*

where exactly the visual effects will appear and for how long. "I said, 'This is supposed to take a long, painful time. This is not one of those shots where it gets shot at and explodes. This is going to be the longest shot you've ever done, just in terms of duration.'"

To get the tension and tragedy of the *Prometheus'* destruction to hit the right note, VFX supervisor Michelle Comens and her team were called upon to pull something very special out of their hats. "Our VFX team is top notch," adds Kindler, who was very pleased with the outcome of the scene. "Rob, Michelle Comens and I had many detailed discussions about how the satellite would look, how it would fire and the damage it would inflict.

"Troublingly, no one felt at all guilty about destroying a ship that had been a stalwart friend of the team since season six!"

Any such potential guilt was surely assuaged by the finished episode, which for both Robert Cooper and Damian Kindler was well executed in both script and finish. "That one worked out great," smiles Cooper. "In the aftermath of 'Icon', we also wanted to see what happens now that the Goa'uld have gone. There are all these planets out there in these weird transitional stages. What happens when the Priors go in there and start pressing buttons? And that was a great opportunity to get in the middle of something and have the *Prometheus* get screwed. It's a really well-directed episode."

"It was great going back and thinking about all the changes that the planet had undergone since Soren's death, [and] since the Priors had come," agrees Kindler. "I really enjoyed working with Ken Girotti, who is a great director and a hell of a guy. Also, Matthew Bennett is great as Kane, too, and I was glad to see him reprise the role." Λ

Off the Grid

Written by: Alan McCullough
Directed by: Peter DeLuise

Guest Cast: Eric Breker (Colonel Reynolds), Maury Chaykin (Nerus), Martin Christopher (Captain Marks), Vince Corazza (Worrel), Matthew Glave (Colonel Paul Emerson), Cliff Simon (Ba'al), Eric Steinberg (Netan), Michael Sunczyk (Vi'tak)

SG-1 visit P6G-452 to investigate an addictive plant called kassa. At first they think it may be propagated by the Ori, but discover that it's actually being farmed and distributed by the Lucian Alliance, a group that has taken the opportunity to step into the gap left by the Goa'uld and are using kassa addiction as a way of keeping their people compliant. After failing to convince the Alliance agents that they are potential buyers for the substance, SG-1 are forced to make a run for it — but the Stargate disappears before their eyes, apparently beamed elsewhere by Asgard technology. The Lucian Alliance rounds them up, holding them responsible. When SG-1 don't check in, Landry sends the *Odyssey* to the planet, and learns from the Tok'ra that other gates are also missing. Confronting the still-imprisoned Nerus, Landry discovers that Ba'al is behind the thefts. He plans to build a new empire somewhere out of Earth's reach. Landry plants a tracking device and a latent virus on the prisoner and allows himself to be persuaded to secure his release. The *Odyssey* rescues SG-1 as they are about to be executed, and the ship traces Nerus' signal. Carter's plan is to locate the seven gates they know are missing and, using a mobile transmitter, beam them beyond Ba'al's shields when the virus Nerus is carrying activates. SG-1 board the vessel carrying the gates, but discover twelve gates rather than the expected seven. They don't have enough transmitters. Trapped and under fire from Ba'al's forces, the *Odyssey* commander, Colonel Emerson, tries to stall for time — without success. Ba'al succeeds in venting the virus and raises his shields, but the Lucian Alliance open fire, wanting to retrieve their missing gates. Emerson retreats to Earth, to discover that SG-1 have beaten him home, having used one of Ba'al's gates to escape the onslaught.

Nerus: My old friend — you wound me deeply.
Ba'al: I'm capable of wounding you much more deeply.

After 'Prototype' and 'Stronghold', Alan McCullough found himself once again charged with interweaving older storylines with SG-1's struggle

Above: The SG-1
team — still as
strong as ever.

against new enemies for 'Off the Grid'. "I pitched that there was a Goa'uld
system lord — not Ba'al, someone else — stealing Stargates,"
McCullough explains, of his original pitch. "The whole Lucian Alliance
thing was brought in after the fact. We were breaking it and Rob Cooper
wanted to do a story with the Lucian Alliance involved in drugs.
He couldn't figure out a story to fit it with, and we thought this might be
the one."

"You can't just have one baddie," says Robert Cooper. "The Lucian
Alliance are an example of yet another group of people — they parallel the
Genii in *Stargate: Atlantis.*"

For McCullough, 'Off the Grid' proved a little easier than writing his
first, 'Prototype', but it was still a tough challenge. Since this time he was
on staff, however, he had the assistance of every other writer and producer in the *Stargate SG-1* offices. "It's very difficult — I think the stages

of writing a script go from hardest to easiest," he says. "Some may disagree, but coming up with the original idea is quite difficult, and breaking the story and fleshing it out to the whole five acts and all the different beats is probably hardest of all, and then from then on writing it all and writing a script gets easier and easier as time goes on. But it's certainly a lot easier when everybody is there. You can try out ideas and say, 'Well, what about this?' And somebody can shoot it down right away. Whereas if you're alone... Back in Toronto, I would have to think of something and carry it through for three days before being told, 'You know what, I don't think this is going to work.' So it's just faster and more efficient to have everybody on set. But even on set, you don't always get that luxury. You still have to work out a story on your own and then just get some general help."

The changes made to the script through the various drafts gave the production the opportunity to bring back Ba'al, the Goa'uld who just won't die no matter how many times he takes a staff blast — particularly true now that he's found a way of cloning himself to create maximum chaos in the galaxy. Ba'al first appeared in the season six episode 'Abyss', when he was responsible for torturing Jack O'Neill. The actor behind him, Cliff Simon, made such an impression on producers and crew alike that the character has endured long after lesser Goa'uld have bitten the dust. "I love Cliff Simon," says Peter DeLuise, who directed the episode. "I'm a huge fan of his and I hope his character's not dead. He's got a lot of clones out there! I'm always excited to work with Cliff, and I did a one-shot that I was particularly proud of [in 'Off the Grid']. I'd just done 'Ripple Effect', so this was a great opportunity to try something really difficult with twinning. He walks over to himself and hands himself a goblet of wine. I was thrilled that we were able to pull that off. That is not an easy thing to do."

Worrel: In fact if you tell me the location of the Stargate, I'm prepared to release you.
Mitchell: Oh, you are not! I can't... [turns to the team] Can you believe he just said that?

Costume designer Christine Mooney reports that Peter DeLuise also had fun with other aspects of filming the episode too — particularly with the civilian clothes SG-1 donned in order to blend in undercover on P6G-452. "It was funny," recalls Mooney, "because the way Peter DeLuise shot that one, it was a bit tongue in cheek I think. He called it the 'butt

Above: *Mr Shaft and associates...*

show' because there they all were, our beautiful actors, in tight leather pants, and I'm sure he trained the camera on that, too!" she laughs.

The costumes gave Mooney the chance to design something a little different for the SG-1 team to wear. Some of the costumes had been hired from a costume hire company, and had originally been created for the Kevin Costner blockbuster movie *Waterworld*. Others were created by Mooney's team. "That one was hilarious to do," Mooney adds, "because the actors are so beautiful. I got to put Amanda in leather pants and corset, and it looked rough and ready and sexy and strong — and she's such a great actress, I was happy to do that. We actually brought some costumes up from Los Angeles and used those in the background. But we created all the boys, the SG-1 team and some of the background stuff as well." Å

The Scourge

Written by: Joseph Mallozzi &
Paul Mullie
Directed by: Ken Girotti

Guest Cast: Tony Alcantar (Dr Myers), Guy Fauchon
(Pullman), Andy Maton (Chapman), Jason McKinnon
(Walker), Mark Oliver (LaPierre), Robert Picardo (Richard
Woolsey), John Prowse (Colonel Pearson), Tamlyn Tomita
(Shen Xiaoyi)

S G-1 are about to embark on an expedition when Landry recalls them
to accompany the International Oversight Advisory, among them
Richard Woolsey, on their first tour of the Gamma Site. The tour
begins well, and Agent Myers introduces the team to an alien bug
responsible for destroying numerous crops on planets recently visited by
Priors. The tour moves on, but Myers suddenly makes a breakthrough —
the bug is carnivorous. And when they eat meat, they reproduce.
Vociferously. So vociferously, in fact, that they break out of containment.
Myers is bitten, and collapses. His body becomes a nursery for the bugs,
which soon overtake the Gamma Site. With the gateroom closed off,
Colonel Pearson orders SG-1 to help retake it while his men take the IOA
to the surface, but Woolsey overrides him — SG-1 came to escort the IOA
and he insists they keep them safe. SG-1 take the IOA above ground,
heading for an unmanned research station ten kilometers through dense
forest. The bugs follow them, sensing them from beneath the ground.
They head for some caves, since the bugs can't burrow through rock.
Trapped in the cave, SG-1 will eventually run out of bullets, Pearson's
team is incommunicado, probably dead, and they have no way of establishing contact with Earth as the planet's atmosphere blocks communication. At SGC, Dr Lee works on a toxin that the *Odyssey* will launch from
orbit — any humans not evacuated will die too. While Carter and Jackson
stay with the IOA, Teal'c and Mitchell head for the F-302s, but the
Gamma Site self-destructs, taking the F-302s — and the Stargate — with
it. Teal'c and Mitchell make their way back to the cave with the bugs stalk-
ing them all the way. All they can do now is wait for the *Odyssey*, but
Carter knows about the toxin. They must find a way of letting the *Odyssey*
know they're alive and on the planet, but to do that they have to reach the
research station. They succeed, and Carter manages to contact the ship —
which beams them all to safety just before the bugs swarm the station.

*Opposite: Once
again, bugs spoil
SG-1's day.*

Mitchell: Sir, I don't mean to gripe...
Landry: Permission to gripe granted.

The Scourge

'The Scourge' represented one of the first true out-and-out team 'shoot-'em-ups' of season nine, as SG-1 find themselves unexpectedly going up against some really nasty alien bugs.

"It's just sort of a monster episode," says co-writer and executive producer Joseph Mallozzi. "A couple of years ago, Rob [Cooper] pitched an idea where the Alpha Site is attacked by these creatures that seed the planet with hatchlings, and they are hunting down the personnel on the base. We ended up marrying that to an idea that I had, which was a fish-out-of-water story where SG-1 is put on baby-sitting duty when the IOA representatives and Woolsey decide to take the first trip off-world."

"Joe pitched this a long time ago," Cooper adds. "He said, 'We have to take the international committee off-world and get them into some trouble.' It was just a question of what that trouble would be."

The trouble begins with the illustrious SG-1, flagship team of Stargate Command, being forced to take the IOA on a tour of the project's research site. "SG-1 is complaining about it and saying, 'Oh my god, we're on baby-sitting duty. I can't believe that they're sending us on this mission.' Of course, they go and while they're on this seemingly mundane mission all hell breaks loose and suddenly they find themselves having to protect these IOA representatives who obviously never expected to be possible bug food!"

Carter: They must be using their echo location as a means to hunt their prey.
Daniel: Us. She means us.

The episode was a chance to have guest actor Robert Picardo return to the show in the guise of international committee leader Richard Woolsey. Having been a part of the show since season seven, ex-*Star Trek: Voyager* star Picardo is clearly a firm favorite with producers, writers and actors alike. "I always love having Bob Picardo on the show," says Mallozzi. "He's always solid. He does a great job with the character, and he always adds little things that just make the character essential. There's this one little instant where they're on the run near the end of the episode, trying to get to this communications station. They end up alerting the bugs, and Mitchell's like, 'Everybody, to the tent!' People start hurrying to the tent, and out of nowhere comes the Woolsey character, his arms pumping, outpacing everyone to get to the tent!" Mallozzi laughs. "It's just little touches like that that really make an episode."

"To have Robert Picardo back was great," agrees Amanda Tapping. "I

Above: No really, they always stand like that.

just love working with him. But the other wacky characters — the French diplomat, he was hilarious, he was so over the top. It was a fun, running, shoot-'em-up. Carter was kind of a bitch to these diplomats by the end, especially the French guy, because she was so sick of them," the actress laughs. "We shot it on location, way out [of town], and everyone just hung out and talked. To have that many actors on set and to be able to sit around and talk was fantastic. It was one of those episodes where it was hard work, and it was outside — it's always more tiring when you're shooting outside — but it was just fun because we had all these new faces on set and new actors to react to."

Although 'The Scourge' mostly feels like a standalone episode, it does connect firmly with the larger Ori arc and storyline. "Originally when it was pitched out, the bugs really had nothing to do with the Ori," Mallozzi explains, "but we decided to give it a tweak at the outline stage."

"We had done the plague in 'The Fourth Horseman', and I started thinking, 'Okay, what's the next thing the Ori would unleash? How else besides disease could the Ori attack?'" Robert Cooper recalls. "It actually came out of 'Off the Grid'. If the Lucian Alliance were keeping people under the thumb with these crops, a good way to undermine that would be to create a pest. So 'The Scourge' happened as a result of the Ori attacking planets through these bugs and removing their food supply and us going, 'Hey, maybe this is a way to fight the Lucian Alliance.' Of course, as usual, we get in a little over our heads and don't quite understand what we are messing with!" Å

Arthur's Mantle

Written by: Alan McCullough
Directed by: Peter DeLuise

Guest Cast: Eric Breker (Colonel Reynolds), Morris Chapdelaine (Prior), Jarvis George (Volnek), Darren Giblin (Conway), Tony Todd (Lord Haikon), Doug Wert (Major Hadden)

Carter is working on a device recovered from Glastonbury when Mitchell interrupts her. Activating the device, the pair find they are out of phase — they can interact with each other, but not with anyone or anything at Stargate Command. Meanwhile, a coded message arrives from the Sodan. When Mitchell and Carter don't answer a summons by Landry, SGC realizes that they are missing. Teal'c accompanies SG-12 to the Sodan's planet while the Stargate Command staff trace Mitchell and Carter's movements. Teal'c discovers that the Sodan have been attacked. Lord Haikon is dying, but reveals that Volnek was responsible for the carnage. Teal'c finds out that Volnek is using a personal cloaking device, and has sabotaged the teleport so they can't escape. Dr Lee examines the Glastonbury device and finds traces of stray lepton radiation, reminding Daniel of the crystal skull. He suggests there should be something on Carter and Mitchell's side to enable them to communicate. Sure enough there's a keyboard, but Daniel has to help them translate. Teal'c uses a cloak, determined to take Volnek down. Earth receives word that Teal'c's party is out of contact, and Mitchell decides to go through the gate to see if he can help. Teal'c finds Volnek, but is wounded. Lord Haikon tells Teal'c that a Prior transformed Volnek into a murderous monster. Dr Lee thinks he's found a way to bring Mitchell and Carter back, but only succeeds in pushing Daniel into the other dimension. Mitchell arrives on the planet with SG teams 22 and 23, who all find themselves trapped. He decides to go after Volnek and realizes that, while cloaked, Teal'c can see him. Daniel figures out the device, but he's not sure it'll help Mitchell, since he's so far away. Unfortunately, it does, and Mitchell reverts to visibility and vulnerability with Volnek closing in and cloaked. Teal'c manages to shoot Volnek, and Mitchell is saved — and solid.

Mitchell: You know, the whole point of my coming here was for me to rescue you.
Teal'c: You are most welcome, Colonel Mitchell.

'Arthur's Mantle' was in some ways a return to a traditional-style *Stargate SG-1* episode. Indeed it even referenced season three episode

'Crystal Skull', in which Daniel Jackson found himself separated from the rest of the world after an encounter with an alien device. For director Peter DeLuise, one of the major challenges of such an episode is finding different techniques to tell the action of the story. "It was 'Crystal Skull', because they were out of phase, and it was [season seven's] 'Evolution, Part II', because you had the zombie technology, and on top of that 'Babylon', because they were using their invisibility shields," explains DeLuise. "So we had this complex thing of them being out of phase, but when you're out of phase you can only be seen

Above: Teal'c's ready for trouble.

by people who are also invisible. But, even though you can be seen, you still can't be touched, so that was a little bit complicated. When you're invisible you have to be able to see stuff, but it has to be different so the audience knows that they're in 'invisible land' and not 'out-of-phase land'. That became a little bit tricky."

DeLuise also had to tackle the idea that Carter, Mitchell and, later, Daniel, were all in a dimension where nothing is solid — except the floor, of course. "It's the old 'pass your hand through the cup' shot," explains the director. "The problem with that is we always do that, and people always walk through each other, and it was, 'Well, what can we do now? We've got to do something different.' So I got it into my head that Mitchell would fall into the table, into the centre island, and that would be a fun way of doing it differently. So he goes to lean on the table, forgetting that he's out of phase with it, and of course he falls through it. When he gets back up, the only thing poking out of the table is his head. We had a lot of fun with that, that was a new way of doing that trick."

Alan McCullough, who wrote the episode, particularly enjoyed penning the script. It was his fourth for *Stargate SG-1*, and each story he had produced for the show had further solidified his place on the writing team. "I guess what I liked about writing 'Arthur's Mantle' is by then I thought I had a good grasp of Mitchell's voice," says the writer, "and in that story, Mitchell is a large part of both what happens on Earth originally, when he goes out of phase with Carter, and also when he goes to the Sodan planet and interacts with Teal'c. I could hear his voice, and he was carrying a lot of that story."

Dr Lee: Okay, umm, I'm going to try to make an adjustment to the algorithm... It's a bit of a long shot...
Landry: You better be sure about this, doctor, because if you make me disappear, there won't be a dimension safe enough for you!

For both writer and director, 'Arthur's Mantle' represented an episode of which they were proud; DeLuise for the innovations he was able to present and McCullough for the continuing development of his own writing in relation to *Stargate SG-1* as a whole. Though there are various things that the director himself would have added — in particular, a rather non-PC scene he would have included for the star of the show! "If I had to do it again, I'd have Mitchell go into the girls' locker room or something," says DeLuise with a grin, "something where he's not supposed to be there. Really take

advantage of the fact that he's so bored he's going to make something happen that is some sort of childish prank, which he didn't really investigate. But he did use it for good because he went to help Teal'c with his mission."

For DeLuise, the light-hearted side of an out-of-phase storyline is one of the joys of producing an episode like this. "I like the silliness," he says. "I like the being able to scream at people who can't hear you and passing your hand through stuff, and people walking through each other, and being able to scream nonsense at people and they can't hear you. To me, that's fun."

For McCullough, the real beauty of 'Arthur's Mantle' was the realization that he was beginning to find his own place on the writing team. "You obviously like it when the lines that you write end up on the screen," says McCullough, "and I think for 'Arthur's Mantle' a lot more of the lines that I wrote personally ended up on the screen, versus being replaced by other writers along the road. So as far as season nine goes, I was able to get more and more of what I conceived on the screen. My instincts were getting better along the way."

DeLuise also stresses what a pleasure it was to work with new leading man Ben Browder on season nine. "Ben's contribution this season has just been so great," enthuses the director. "I'm a huge fan of his, and I love his energy and what he brings to the show. I think that's important [to say], because it's a terribly difficult job, and they are huge shoes he's got to fill. It's important to me that somebody says something nice about Ben, because he works his ass off." Λ

Above: Sometimes, all you can do is wait.

Crusade

Written by: Robert C. Cooper	Guest Cast: Doug Abrahams (Prior), Gary Chalk
Directed by: Robert C. Cooper	(Colonel Chekov), Alex Dafoe (Halstrom), Daniella
	Evangelista (Denya), Tim Guinee (Tomin), Michael
	Ironside (Seevis), Dan Shea (Sergeant Siler), Tamlyn
	Tomita (Shen Xiaoyi)

A pregnant Vala visits the SGC, but not as herself — rather, in the body of Daniel, which she is inhabiting. She has important news for Landry, though the General would rather have Daniel back — they are supposed to be meeting with the Russian and Chinese delegates of the international committee. Vala explains what has happened to her over the past months. She was found in the village of Ver Isca and looked after by a crippled young man called Tomin. Vala tried to contact the anti-Ori resistance, and married Tomin to cover her unlawful pregnancy, which occurred out of wedlock, though she doesn't know how. However, Tomin, who is a devout worshipper of the Ori, has been persuaded to join their crusade as a warrior after the local Prior healed his leg. During her story, Landry is called away to the meeting and is told by the Russian, Chekov, that his country is withdrawing their support — and taking back their Stargate. Vala continues her story, in which she is captured by a local Ori informer as she tries to find the resistance, and is left tied out in the elements until she confesses her sins. Tomin abandons her, afraid of his attachment to her. After three days both Vala and her baby have survived, and Tomin rescues her before he and the other crusaders leave for training. She follows and sees a fleet of Ori ships, ready to attack. The resistance planned to stop the crusade by killing the village's Ori followers in one go during a demonstration of the ships, but the attempt failed. Vala believes the Ori have a working Supergate and are preparing a mass invasion. Suddenly, Daniel returns to normal and SG-1 realize something must have happened to Vala. Tomin has returned, and now knows that the baby is not his, though a Prior tells him that the pregnancy is the will of the Ori. To save herself, Vala convinces Tomin that the child is a miracle and he must save her by taking her with him on the invasion fleet. Meanwhile, Stargate Command knows the attack is coming, and begin to search for possible sites where it could occur...

Vala: By the looks on your faces I can see you're not surprised I had more in common with the village harlot than I did with any of the ladies of the local knitting circle.

Above: Vala finds
herself in an un-
expected situation.

The penultimate episode of the season, which saw the much-anticipated return of Claudia Black's character Vala and an increased urgency for the SG-1 team, was both written and directed by *Stargate SG-1*'s executive producer and show runner, Robert C. Cooper.

"It was a lot of fun," Cooper says with a smile. "Everybody kept asking me, 'Are you prepared, are you prepared, are you prepared?' And I felt like the Jaffa on the bridge, every time the Goa'uld say 'prepare to fire' — 'I'm not doing anything but standing here — I'm prepared to fire! I'm ready to go!' I've been ready to direct for a long, *long* time, I just haven't had the time. My other job of writing and producing forty episodes of television has kind of got in the way," he jokes. "But it just turned out that the end of the season is the perfect time, and it was the one thing that I hadn't tackled yet. It was an element of the creative process that I really wanted to participate in, and I had a great time doing it. I always did have an appreciation for the directors on the show, what they do and how they do it, and the actors and what they do. But doing it [yourself] gives you a whole different level of appreciation."

The story itself was very ambitious and needed to successfully juggle many vital elements. For a start, Cooper needed to re-introduce the character of Vala and explain exactly where she has been for most of the past season. "When you tell a story in flashback, as a voice over, it always gives you a tremendous amount of freedom," explains the executive producer. "It's dangerous, because you can do it very badly, in which case it is all exposition. If you do it well, you have the opportunity to tell a lot of story and get to know characters much better in a very short period of time. What we had to do was tell what's happened to Vala over the last nine months in one episode, so of course it was going to get condensed. There were a lot of very big ideas that needed to be grounded. She couldn't just say, 'I got married,' and not understand why she had to do that."

Carter: Well, since you disintegrated the Alteran communication stones and the base terminal in the kawoosh, we've been...
Mitchell: I'm sorry, the *what*?

In explaining Vala's most recent adventures, Cooper had the opportunity to explore a different perspective to the story he had spent a year weaving. "This episode could have been called 'The Other Side'," he says. "We tend to only see things from our own perspective. When we look at things like terrorism, we just see these one-dimensional bad guys that strap bombs to themselves. But I think the most interesting documentary pieces that I've seen have been from people who have been embedded in those cultures. Why do they believe what they do, and how do we change that? *Can* we change that? And when you get to see how these people think and why they are doing what they are doing, it creates a multi-dimensional situation, not just 'good guys and bad guys'. The character of Tomin, whom Vala has married, is a very interesting character for me. He's a guy who is a wonderful, sweet man whom we should love, who is also willing to kill in the name of what he believes in, which is on some levels admirable. In our fictional world of *Stargate SG-1*, he's unfortunately misinformed. It's all about which side you happen to fall on and what you believe in. But that power of belief in dictating your actions is a very interesting thing to explore. I hope that the pregnancy aspect of the story doesn't overshadow that part of the story."

With 'Crusade', *Stargate SG-1* again courted controversy with its

Above: Vala has a lot of explaining to do.

portrayal of Vala's 'virgin' conception. Having already raised eyebrows with the overtly religious aspects of the Ori storyline early in the season, Cooper prepared to close the show's year with an equally fiery topic for the critics to debate.

"We really didn't have a choice," says Cooper. "Sci Fi asked us to bring Vala back. The pregnancy was something that got added into the story because Claudia was actually pregnant, and it seemed to ultimately fit. The issue, once again, of potentially drawing a little closely to religious story lines is one that we obviously talked about, and were concerned about. The fact is, Christianity is not unique in its belief in [such a] conception. In the script, there is a reference to Darth Vader! We figured if they can do it in the new *Star Wars* trilogy, we can do it! Everyone accuses me of ripping off *Star Wars* all the time anyway," he says with a laugh. "It just gave Claudia so many wonderful things to play, and Vala once again is going to be a richer character for this story."

Despite the controversy surrounding his directorial début, Cooper reports that overall, it was a wonderful experience. "It's always a compromise," he acknowledges. "There are only eight days to shoot the show. You'd love to get this shot or that shot and do another one. [But] we compromise as writers all the time. The show has a particular budget that you have to stick to, and the hours are very, very hard — but it's also a whole lot of fun. Everyone talked about how happy I was, walking onto the set. I was on cloud nine! And I was grateful for everybody's support too, they were all really positive, and I think everybody tried a little harder. Hopefully I didn't screw it up too badly!" Å

Camelot

Written by: Joseph Mallozzi & Paul Mullie Directed by: Martin Wood	Guest Cast: Gary Chalk (Colonel Chekov), Martin Christopher (Major Marks), Noah Danby (Cha'ra), Trevor Devall (voice of Kvasir), Connor Crash Dunn (Ramus), Matthew Glave (Colonel Paul Emerson), Katharine Isabelle (Valencia), John Noble (Meurik), Eric Steinberg (Netan), David Thomson (Antonius), Matthew Walker (Merlin)

Searching for Merlin's weapon, SG-1 arrive at a village, Camelot, which has its own sword-in-the-stone. The village leader, Meurik, welcomes them, and explains that they are waiting for the arrival of Arthur. Merlin's library is sealed and supposedly protected by a curse — another knight. One of the villagers goes against Meurik's wishes and shows SG-1 the library, but the knight is triggered and attacks the villager and his wife. Meurik orders the team to leave just before they are retrieved by Colonel Pendergast of the *Odyssey*, who tells them that another Ori Supergate has been located. Daniel and Mitchell beam back down into the library while Carter heads off with the ship and Teal'c goes to ask the Lucian Alliance to help. Mitchell is forced to fight the knight again, but isn't as successful this time. Daniel, after listening to a holographic Merlin, is unable to find a cut-off, and shoots the crystals of the holographic chamber, destroying the knight. However, the hologram has pointed Daniel towards a ruby stone. Could it be the key to Merlin's weapon? The *Odyssey* is joined by the Asgard Kvasir, who thinks he knows what the weapon is — something that will feed interference into the Ascended plane. However, Daniel and Mitchell can't find the jewel. Meurik gives them the names of three planets that may have the bloodstone, and Mitchell and Jackson depart on the *Korolev*. Carter suggests they should dial out on the Supergate, to try and prevent the Ori dialing in, and takes a spacewalk to do just that. But the Ori dial in before she can succeed and the resulting energy surge disrupts the magnetic lock on her suit, causing her to drift unsecured into space. The Supergate opens and the Ori fleet appears, firing as a huge battle starts. Vala, aboard one of the Ori ships, and heavily pregnant, can only watch…

Teal'c: Given your narrow victory over the knight in the Avalon cave, it would seem that your over-confidence is ill advised.

Mitchell: Did I say anything about me doing the fighting?

After a year such as the one *Stargate SG-1* was about to wrap up, only the biggest bang of an episode could do justice to the huge story that the team of writers and producers had begun to tell. As the writing of 'Camelot' got underway, it had already been decided that the season would end on a cliffhanger — despite the fact that no one was as yet sure whether the SG-1 team would be returning to screens the following year.

"We got tired of ending the show," Robert Cooper says with a laugh. "We've done it the best we can now, with [season eight's] 'Moebius'. That was the best we could do. That's the ending! Now we're starting something new, and you don't end a series at the end of season one. People like the cliffhangers. It gets people eager for next season!"

Charged with penning the finale was writing and producing duo Joseph Mallozzi and Paul Mullie, who found themselves with the task of ending the year without knowing what would happen in the future.

Above: Mitchell regrets opting for the mud bath with extra edge.

"I had an idea where some things would end up, but to be honest I had no idea where other things would [go]," Mallozzi confesses. "At the end, when Vala is looking out and she sees that one of our ships is destroyed, and you don't really know what ship it is — it could either be the *Korolev* or the *Odyssey*. And depending on things like, for example, if all of our actors wanted to come back [for a tenth season], it would go one way, if maybe some of our actors decided they wanted to do something else, then it would have gone another way. So this was another episode where we were juggling a little bit. The challenge was giving something for all of the characters to do. So you've got Mitchell stepping up and dealing with the knight, you've got Daniel doing his research, you've got Carter on the space gate, you've got Teal'c dealing with the Lucian Alliance. These types of episodes are satisfying to write, but also very challenging in that there's a lot of moves. Who's doing what and when? It's a puzzle that you have to put together at the outline stage. When it works, it's great. I think it *did* work. It's a great season finale."

Daniel: Clearly it can't be a weapon in the conventional sense. See, the Ascended beings transcend space/time as we know it. This device would have to do the same thing.
Mitchell: In other words, you have no idea what it might be.

"I really liked the way it turned out," agrees director Martin Wood, though he goes on to qualify his statement. "The thing you always miss as a director is time. When you sit down to block out a script, you always have more time than you actually have to shoot! This is what the writer wants, this is what you ultimately come up with, and this is what you really want to do with it. And those three things you juggle — here's what's expected of you, here's what your time is going to give you and here's what you'd love to do. When I do a shot list, I always call it a 'dream sheet'; if I have the time to do it, this is what I really want to do. I have *never* had the time to shoot a dream sheet. 'Camelot' is one of those shows where I know what it could have been if I'd had another day or two. And 'could have beens' don't mean anything! Even what I did shoot didn't show up on there sometimes, but it's a better show for not having all the extra stuff that I was going to put into it, I think."

One aspect of the original script that was altered for shooting was the style of Mitchell's fight with the Black Knight. According to the original script, the knight was to have been battling Mitchell from a vantage point on a warhorse. In the event, Wood decided to scrap that element, as he

Above: Sam and Daniel consider their options.

explains. "It would have become an entirely different fight if the Black Knight had been on a horse. Even though there would have been an element of coolness to it, it would not have recalled 'Avalon'. I think that's an important call back, to go back to 'Avalon' with that [scene], because in 'Avalon' he was victorious and now he's not. Against someone on a war horse, it's a completely different fight, and I didn't think that was necessary. It was a money thing, about affording a horse fight and saying 'Okay, do we *need* that?' If we'd had a full day to shoot just this sword fight, we would have been fine, but we were not going to have that luxury."

The final scenes of 'Camelot' involve some of the most stunning VFX shots ever seen in *Stargate SG-1*. For actress Amanda Tapping, filming Carter's reaction to the devastation around her involved bobbing up and down on a boom in her space suit.

"That's hard," Tapping says with a chuckle. "You totally forget how hard it is to be in front of a green screen and have the director yell, 'And the ship goes overhead, and a bomb goes off to your left!' and you're trying desperately to make it real. It's really a struggle to not go over the top with it, but to pay due heed to what's happening. A massive battle is going on around her while she's floating in space, it's pretty bizarre. The process was fun. Getting in and out of that space suit is not much fun... that's *not* a comfortable thing to be wearing! But when you see it all put together, you go, 'Oh wow! That's pretty cool!'" Å

You know, I've read your mission reports on the Asgard, and
  they're not what I was expecting.
What were you expecting?
Well, pants for one...

Stargate SG-1 has a long history of 'twinning' or 'double' episodes,
where characters that the audience is accustomed to seeing find
themselves face to face with — well, themselves! This tradition
started with season one's 'Tin Man', in which the lonely survivor of
a technologically advanced race cloned the team's consciousnesses.
Having downloaded them into robotic versions of themselves, he intended to keep them as companions and helpmates. Next, 'There But For the
Grace of God' established the theory of parallel universes, which would
eventually, in 'Point of No Return', see some of the team meeting themselves once more. In latter seasons, episodes such as 'Gemini' provided
an outlet for the show to take advantage of the advanced technology to
create increasingly elaborate twinning shots. However, with the arrival of
the script for 'Ripple Effect', it became apparent that the show could try
its most complicated twin episode yet — and really test the advances
made by camera technology.

Upon reading 'Ripple Effect', a plot crowded with multiple duplicates
of the SG-1 team, Peter DeLuise, who was charged with making Joseph
Mallozzi and Paul Mullie's script into a reality, saw the opportunity for a
real challenge, and decided to push it to the very limits. "Really good
twinning involves never letting the audience go, 'Oh, that's so fake, it's so
obvious that this half of the screen is devoted to this character and that
half of the screen is devoted to that character,'" says DeLuise. "Tell-tale
signs of a bad twinning [are]: they're not touching each other, they're not
overlapping and they're not really hearing each other — they're not even
looking at each other! Usually it's two people in dead profile, which also
seems to be really flat and uninteresting. So what we were trying to do
was create depth by having raking shots."

A raking shot is where the focus is pulled on the person standing in
front, but the shot also shows the person standing in the background,
allowing what is seen by the audience in the finished cut to suggest distance and depth between the two people. As a result the finished shot is
much more believable than if, say, the two characters had been standing
side by side on a flat plane — although to do the former is a far more

Above: *Carter is determined not to notice the absence of pants.*

complicated procedure. "A lot of times, the silhouette of the one in the front is going to overlap the one in the back," DeLuise explains. "That starts to create a problem. We can't just cut the frame in half and have one on one side and one on the other, because there's no actual way to delineate. You have to be able to cut out the silhouette of the one in front. You usually do that by photographing that one over a green or blue [screen], and the computer is able to cut out that image and put it over whatever you want it put on. The reason we do that is if we don't, someone has to do it by hand, and that is *so* time consuming. That's called rotoscoping, and you *never* want to do that. It involves an actual person tracing the outline on every single frame of film. And it never looks as good, because you have human error."

Prior to the technological advances of the past few years, twinning would have relied on rotoscoping to provide some link between the two spliced frames, and would also have involved a camera locked in position to make sure that any interaction that the two (or more) characters had would match up on both sides of the finally edited frame. For 'Ripple Effect', DeLuise would still be using a locked-off camera, but it would in fact move. Instead of remaining in one position at all times, this moving lock-off would follow a recorded motion, allowing DeLuise to film multiple passes of a scene — a separate 'pass' for each duplicate character in the scene. "The image is exactly the same and it moves in exactly the same way," elaborates the director, "so you can put duplicate images of

Above: Shooting the scene where Carter pours coffee for Carter, while Dr Lee (Bill Dow) explains his theory to Carter...

the same thing in a moving picture. That's why it's such a wonderful tool for a twinning episode."

With the equipment in place to create an episode with extensive twinning opportunities, DeLuise was able to create particularly challenging scenes, such as Carter in a room with around fifteen different versions of herself. Though the director confesses that the scene as filmed ended up being a lot more complicated and time-consuming than originally intended in the script, mainly because DeLuise himself was determined to be as ambitious as possible during the shoot!

"The 'seventeen Carters' one was the most difficult of the shots," DeLuise confesses. "It was hardest for Amanda Tapping! What we did was create a space we knew we would be able to have a lot of Carters in. That required that if she moved by or in front of a place where she was going to be later, there needed to be green screen behind her. So rather than try to figure out [whether] there was an overlap between this Carter and that Carter, we just made the whole back all green screen. My first thought was to have an enormous conference room desk in the middle of the room, almost like the Last Supper, where we'd have all the Carters there like the Apostles! Then, as that idea began to expand, I said, 'Well, we can have foreground Carters and background Carters even behind that.' We didn't have to limit ourselves, because I think in the story at that point they had mentioned that seventeen different versions of SG-1 had come through

the gate. So I said we'd go for seventeen — and I think, if you count them very carefully, that you'll find that I might have gone over," he says with a laugh. "I just kept putting Carters into the background."

Even though it took an entire day to shoot and required actress Amanda Tapping to shoot multiple versions of the same scene, DeLuise still used photo doubles to make it a little easier. "If anybody is facing away from the camera, then they're not really Amanda Tapping. Unless you can see their eyes, or at least part of their eyes, then it's not actually her."

To increase the audience's investment in the episode and help them suspend their disbelief further, DeLuise worked on coming up with moments that would blend together each separate Carter's 'pass'. Some of the interaction was less obvious, glimpsed in the background of the scene, but others were more prominent. "The idea that there would be a Carter handing around coffee was a lot of fun," says DeLuise. "The idea that she would offer herself coffee and then refuse it — none of that was in the script. And at one point, there was a little bit of concern that that scene was taking too long. [But] for me, the reason for doing the episode was to do scenes like that. So I went ahead and did as many Carters as I could! If I had said I had planned on doing seventeen Carters ahead of time, I think they would have tried to stop me," he admits. "That's *way* too many. But what we had planned for was mostly doubles and just a few actual real Carters, and then it turned out to be quite a lot of real

Above: Before: 'green' SG-1 arrives home...

Carters and not a lot of doubles — and that's what took so much time.

"In that particular scene, Amanda Tapping didn't have to learn a lot of lines. In other scenes, she had lines between her selves and she had to learn both parts and be exactly on time. But having her change into all the different outfits [for this scene] was a bit of a handful," DeLuise continues, of another component that further complicated filming. "And because it was already too time consuming, we couldn't really change her hair or add an eye patch or a scar. So there was just a little bit of hair change off-stage, and she would just change her body language. Some of the Carters were a little bit more aggressive, some of them were a little bit more sheepish. We also got in a version of Carter that may or may not have been in [season eight finale] 'Moebius'. There was a possibility that it was the very sheepish, very nerdy shut-in who just eats Jell-O all day. That one scene was complicated, and everyone was very concerned that it took too much time, but I think ultimately a lot of people think it was worth it."

DeLuise also tried to introduce the sense of difference between the teams into other areas of the episode. Although not all the teams that came through the gate had the focus on them, the director still managed to herald alterations in character to illustrate where their own individual environments had influenced them. "There was the one team with the jungle camo, where Teal'c has a big wing gun. That was a choice — I specified that they used a wing gun. I thought that that group was very warlike, and they were perhaps more aggressive than we were because they were in the

Above: ...And after: as 'black' SG-1 looks on.

middle of a very big war. They just looked like they had been through more battles, because the clothing was specified [in the script], I was kind of like, 'Well, that sounds like they are more warlike. So lets just give them all big guns.' As soon as they came through the gate, and they saw all the guys pointing guns at them, their instinct was to point their guns back. We've been through so many adventures where nothing is as it seems, that they go, 'Okay, well, we should probably defend ourselves because we don't know what's going on.'" DeLuise says with a laugh.

To make things a little simpler on himself, and to give the cast and crew a vague hope of keeping a mental grasp on which SG-1 team was which, DeLuise also decided to use a more obvious visual cue. "We color-coded the teams," explains the director. "I asked Joe Mallozzi to put the uniform color of the person that we were dealing with [in the script] every single time. That's why we kept them in their uniforms, so we could differentiate them! So our regular team was 'green', and our bad guy team was 'black'.

"One enormous loophole in the whole thing is that the first group to come back is the black team. They left wearing green and came back wearing black, and nobody said anything? Nobody said, 'Hey, weren't you guys wearing green when you left?'" DeLuise laughs. "Nobody takes notice of the fact that when the next team comes in, they're in green. They are the ones that came from our version of Earth. We made an announcement during the concept meeting, 'Nobody is allowed to mention that,' because it was a giant conceit. The lame excuse was that they left during the nightshift and came back during the dayshift. Maybe they had their different colored outfits in their backpacks, who knows?"

Some of the director's ideas didn't get further than the meeting stage, in particular his suggestion for a resolution to the ongoing joke about Carter's love life. "There were a lot of hints about a relationship for Carter," he says. "Well, obviously they're trying to keep the 'Shippers' happy, although they never did say that. So what I thought was, make it even more ambiguous by having black Carter and black Mitchell have some heat between them. I got shut down for that," he chuckles. "They didn't like the idea! I said, 'Well, you know, in the world of infinite alternatives, it's a possibility, so why not show that? Who cares if black Carter and black Mitchell are having a relationship? That doesn't mean green Carter is having a relationship with green Mitchell!' But I got slapped down for that..."

The tone of 'Ripple Effect' turns decidedly darker when the black-uniformed SG-1 reveal exactly what is going on and why, resulting in SG-1 effectively taking themselves prisoner. This deceptively unassuming scene is complicated by the fact that only half the players in the scene are physically there at any one time. Though in the finished episode, a movement such as this took less than a minute of screen time, it had to be intricately planned. "We had the black SG-1 and the green SG-1 on the bridge, and we needed [them to move]," elaborates the director. "The first group started all the way over on the left and they moved to behind the second group that was all seated. That involved doing close-ups of every single one of them, so each character had to change clothes according to who we were going to shoot. They had to change their shirt and move behind the other person, so there was a lot of clothing changes — and that caused a lot of concerns as well, because that took time."

Suffice it to say that the continuity and costume departments worked overtime during the filming of 'Ripple Effect', in particular on the scenes towards the end of the episode, when some of the alternate SG-1 masquerades as the original team. "Those poor wardrobe people," says DeLuise. "Every new shot was, 'Okay, make a list.' We called them [the original team] the 'realies', the real actors. I'd say, 'Mitchell's in green, Carter's in green, Daniel's in black, Teal'c's in black. Now, our 'fakies': fake Mitchell in black, fake Carter in black, fake Daniel in green, fake Teal'c in green. So you need to have that list.' And they would all get changed into the appropriate outfits, come back, we would film that one shot, and then we would have to change them again, because they had to shoot both sides. It got kind of hectic. It slowed the process down."

A scene containing twins still needs to be paced out and planned in the same manner as a normal scene, DeLuise explains: "You try to block it like it's a normal scene, because if you block it any differently, the audience will say, 'Well, why is it so weird? Why is it so different? Why are they all across the room from each other?' So you pick your moments. Does it make sense for green Daniel and black Daniel to be sitting next to each other in this scene, or would it be better to have them on opposite sides of the room? And should they be sitting next to each other? Should they be standing, or sitting, should one be standing and one sitting? And how will that make the frame look?"

Above: Will the real SG-1 please stand up?

Ultimately, the episode became one of the most memorable examples of the team meeting itself — over and over. For DeLuise, all the hard work and long hours were worth the effort. "Doing a twinning episode, you usually plan on doing way more actual trick shots than you end up doing," he elaborates. "It's just so much slower to do twinning that you end up scrapping stuff, and you have to do that because if you don't manage your time properly, it can be very bad. But we didn't change a lot — Joe and Paul are very good at getting all the points there! At the end of the episode, a lot of people could forget that we didn't use any real twins! They don't really exist on two different planes — there's only one of them in real life!

"It is definitely my favorite one of the year, because of the challenge and how much fun it was to get all the doubles and the cloning [working]. It was a wonderful challenge, and a lot of people have said that it's their favorite episode." Å

General Hank Landry

"A general is only as good as the people he commands."

Stargate SG-1 has always had the ability to attract high-profile guest stars, but with season nine the bar was raised another notch. With the departure of General O'Neill, Stargate Command required a new commander, and Brad Wright and Robert Cooper decided to go all-out and ask veteran actor Beau Bridges to join the team. Happy to accept the regularly recurring role, Bridges immediately showed his enthusiasm for General Hank Landry by creating a detailed past for the character.

"One of the things that impressed me so much about the show at the beginning was that they had all these real air force guys involved [and] appearing on the show," explains Bridges, "including General John Jumper — the highest ranking general at the time. I liked that, and so I felt a sense of responsibility to make sure I'm getting that part of it right. They [the producers] of course had the final say on who this character was going to be, but I immediately got into reading up on American generals — [from] George Washington all the way through. And I just started jotting down character aspects of these people, also things that they had said about different aspects of life. I ended up with about forty or fifty pages of all these quotes from these generals and descriptions about them. Then I began to categorize them into different things, depending on what they were talking about. I ended up with a really interesting document, so I handed that over to the producers and the writers. I felt that they were the guys who were going to be writing the thing, so the information might be more useful to them. Throughout the season, some of that research made it onto the page. I think that they enjoyed that — at least, that's what they told me," laughs the actor, "because it gave them a place to start with the character. They didn't have to dream it up totally out of their heads. That must be a real challenge, to have to do so many of those shows."

The extensive research conducted by Bridges prior to the start of filming gave the actor a completely clear picture of Landry's personality, background and attitude towards his position. Even from his earliest interaction with Ben Browder's Cameron Mitchell, it was clear that Landry had a wicked (if often hidden) sense of humor and, for a man in the latter stages of his military career, the general shows no indication of wishing to slow down in his duties.

"I think he's a fierce competitor, and he enjoys competition — he

enjoys his job. The harder and bigger the battle, the more fun he has, which is kind of weird," Bridges laughs. "He has a very strong sense of family with the people he works with, [though] maybe not such a strong sense with his own family. He has a good sense of what is right and what is wrong, and he can see [through] people pretty quickly. I think he's intrigued with this new challenge in his life — he was ready to retire, and now he's fighting aliens! That's exciting for him."

Stargate SG-1, of course, has a huge and distinctly dedicated fan-base. Bridges reveals that this was also something he considered during his preparation for the role. "It's the most watched science fiction television series of all time," he says simply. "There's a certain responsibility, I think, when you join an effort like that, that's reaching out to people who are so [dedicated]. You can count on these folks, these fans. I went to my first convention in San Diego, and it was so much fun! These people just love the show, and so, as an actor on it, I want to return their generosity, just be there for them and score that touchdown for them. It inspires me."

Certainly, throughout his first year as part of the *Stargate SG-1* universe, Beau Bridges brought many inspired moments to the show — Landry's relationship with his estranged daughter, Dr Lam, for example, or laying down the law for Maury Chaykin's frankly revolting Goa'uld Neu'rus in the episode 'Beachhead'. According to Bridges' own philosophy, good film-making in all its forms is a team activity, and producing *Stargate SG-1* is the perfect reflection of such a method.

"For me, making movies is really such a collaborative effort. I think it's important for people to communicate and talk to each other, so that's what I do, with whoever the other actors are and with the director. Our directors are great — there are about four or five of them that trade off on the episodes, and most of them have been around the show since its beginning, or at least way early on. So they are really a part of the family, and they understand the characters so totally and completely that a lot of it I really give up to the individual directors. The script is always the most important element of telling a story on film. So I like to get comfortable with that, and I go up and will speak to Robert Cooper about anything that I don't understand in the script, or suggest a little change here and there. I try to get that done long before the scene is being shot. Then, when we're in there doing it, it's really about acting."

Though he is for the most part happy to be led by the writers' vision for Hank Landry's future, Bridges confesses that he does have areas he would like to explore. "The universe is just so vast, there must be other worlds out there that we have no idea [about]. What's going to happen

when we need to deal with outside forces, outside the universe that we know? When that happens, hopefully as a human race, we can come together and work together to try and protect ourselves and our planet. Right now, we don't seem to be doing a very good job of that! Our show is first an entertainment — I don't think it's a hugely profound discussion of worldly matters — but on the other hand it is a chance to communicate about the quality of our lives, how we deal with each other and the lack of respect that we have for people of different cultures. I remember reading a bunch of short stories by Ray Bradbury. He wrote that our greatest problem as a human race is an aesthetic one. We can't seem to deal with people that look different and cultures that are different. His point was, what's going to happen when some quivering wiggling mass comes from outer space and stands before us and tries to talk to us? We're not going to be able to communicate, because we can't even deal with people who have a different color skin or a different haircut! It seems to be an aesthetic challenge for us. I think that there is that chance for the stories — and I think you can tell by the stories [our] producers turn out, that they want the audience to have fun, but they're also interested in throwing some [of these] ideas around." Å

Dr Daniel Jackson

"A little less talk, a little more shut the hell up!"

"We've always believed, for the longest time, that this show was much more than the sum of its parts," says Michael Shanks, whose enjoyment of *Stargate SG-1*'s season nine is clear. "The concept of the show was not person-specific, it wasn't even cast-specific, as *Stargate: Atlantis* has proven. There are so many possibilities with this wonderful prop. Anything can happen. It's a great story-telling device for science fiction, and the audience is continuing to enjoy it."

For Shanks, the massive changes that accompanied Richard Dean Anderson's departure for *Stargate SG-1*'s ninth year on air were more to be welcomed than worried about. "A lot of people were really worried, with Rick going, that it would be the end of it all, and it obviously hasn't proven to be true. We've certainly enjoyed the new energy that the new cast has brought, and the fresh ideas and enthusiasm that comes with it. For all of us jaded relics that lie around here," jokes the actor, "it's great to have this different perspective and new energy to put into it. It makes it a completely different show, from our perspective, but it's been a lot of fun this year."

Through the addition of *Stargate SG-1*'s newest cast members, Shanks has found new opportunities to expand on Daniel's character. According to the actor, this has particularly been the case with Vala, played by Claudia Black. Having previously established a humor-filled relationship between the two characters in the season eight episode 'Prometheus Unbound', Shanks and Black were able to expand on their characters' relationship with Black's extended return in season nine.

"Claudia is wonderful," smiles Shanks. "She's such a great talent to work with — it's a real privilege. What I love about what Vala brought out in my character was something that Daniel never got to play before — constant exasperation. Daniel's very used to getting his own way, he's used to breaking people in, and Vala's this perfect foil. She's kind of like the perfect Rubik's Cube for Daniel. He really wants to help her, but she won't allow herself to be helped, and at the same time that intrigues Daniel even further and draws him into the web, where he gets caught up in the frustration. I think he's the same way for her. For her, here's this one guy who doesn't believe her, the one guy she can't pull the wool over his eyes, the one guy she can't fool. And I think that's also fascinating for her character. So it's a wonderful ying/yang relationship, but

there's also a wonderful respect that built as the season evolved. So as much as it was fun to play the banter, there was a certain heart and presence there."

Another relationship that Daniel had to develop from scratch for season nine was with new member and leadership figure Cameron Mitchell. Equally, Shanks and the rest of the existing *SG-1* cast and crew were charged with welcoming actor Ben Browder to the line-up. For Shanks, the addition of Browder fulfilled another role in the team that complimented the ensemble, while the two actors' ability to debate the aspects of a script have added to the two characters' interaction.

"It's fun," says Shanks, of the new addition. "Ben and I, as much as we're similar, we're also recognizing we have a lot of differences. He's very much a guy who, like his character, loves the action stuff! He loves picking up the weapons and tumbling through the forest and getting his butt kicked, fighting and rolling around. As much as I can enjoy that, mostly my character is the voice of the story. So we constantly have different points of view about where we think the story should be, or where the balance is, and I think that's rubbed off on the characters. That layer of antagonism there that is just inevitable between myself and Ben from the different conversations — that's also [the case] with Mitchell and Daniel, in as much as they seem to get along most of the time, but there's this thin layer of antagonism. That comes from our personal relationship and different ideas of the storytelling and where it should sit."

The changes in character dynamic have been more than matched by the changes in the rest of the series, especially the introduction of the Ori. For Daniel Jackson, the advent of the Ori has been of particular significance. "There's a lot that's been based around the character, especially with this new villain," says Shanks. "It's based a lot on what Daniel's thru line has been for the last several years."

Besides being very much connected to the history of the Ancients that Daniel has been investigating since the season one episode 'The Torment of Tantalus', the Ori have also represented a philosophical depth that *Stargate SG-1* hasn't often explored before.

"There have been debates waged on which religion we're trying to represent with the Ori," says the actor, "and I think the best answer that I can give from my perception is that we're not trying to represent any specific religion. It is the fundamentalist concept that I certainly think, in this day and age, is a subject that needs to be addressed. And [it is] something that, if it's put out there in the science fiction metaphor concept, then people will be able to look at it, and be able to ask questions that are harmless, but in the same way are representing something that is being debated on different fronts. It's a good point for what we're trying to debate. The philosophical debate of religion is always a constant. Someone [said] the other day that the Christian right is really pissed off that we're telling this storyline, so we sort of said, 'Well that's no surprise, the Christian right is always pissed off.'" Shanks laughs. "My feeling on the subject has always been that religion seems to cause most of the strife and difficulty in this world, as well as a lot of the goodness as well. You have that double-edged sword that operates in everybody's lives, and in such a strong and emphatic way on a daily basis, that when we bring it up in this, certainly emotions get wrapped up in it. I love it. I certainly think we've got the capacity to delve even further into it. We're on the right track to create a strong philosophical debate on the subject matter." Å

Lieutenant Colonel Cameron Mitchell

"Look, I'll do any crazy exercise you want... within reason."

In the wake of Richard Dean Anderson's departure from *Stargate SG-1*, it was necessary to find an actor of equal weight to plug a gap almost impossible to fill. Anderson's Jack O'Neill was more than just the leader of the SG-1 team, he was the figurehead of the show. Who could the producers find to fill such shoes? The answer came in the shape of another science fiction icon — Ben Browder, former star of long-running science fiction series *Farscape*. It seemed that the actor had it all — serious acting chops, his own very dedicated fanbase, and extensive experience of shooting the science fiction genre. In fact, Browder had been on the producers' list for a guest role, or perhaps even something more permanent, for a while, but had previously not been available. Now, however, the chance arose to bring him aboard. So was born the character of Lieutenant Colonel Cameron Mitchell: SGC pilot, general hot shot and new leader of Stargate Command's flagship team. For Browder, playing the new arrival at SGC — and a 'newbie' to travel through the Stargate — was a refreshing experience.

"It's fun to play, because at the beginning of the year, he's surrounded by characters who have saved the world 160 times," says the actor, "[in a] way, he is kind of back to the roots of the show, in the enthusiasm for getting out there. It's inherently different, obviously, with the departure of Rick. It's not for me to judge if it's successful or not, because I just don't know. Plus, there's a great danger of patting myself on the back, or patting someone else on the back... The arbiter of these things is the audience, not me! I'm always surprised when anything works. Quite frankly, I'm usually lucky to have a job," Browder jokes.

His first year as head of the SG-1 team packed in a lot of new experiences for Mitchell, from the basics of gate travel to battling Earth's new enemy, the Ori.

"A character doesn't exist at points, it exists as a thread running through the cloth. And if you pull one thread, is the whole thing going to unravel?" Browder points out when asked to delineate what he feels are the most important moments for Mitchell in season nine. "There are scenes which I consider to be important in any number of episodes. Obviously, the première is important for the introduction of Mitchell. 'Babylon' is, to a certain degree, important. But particularly after 'Babylon', running through the season, you hope that *every* episode has

something which is important to you personally as an actor, where you go, 'That worked, that's what's this character is about.' You learn that in the process of doing it; in the process of reading the script, acting out the script and seeing the script produced.

"Because television is a different beast from film, the character doesn't exist for two hours, [it] exists for twenty hours per season, potentially existing, in the case of Teal'c, for example, for nine seasons of the show so far. There may be a single moment in a single episode that's important. They get revealed in places of the story which you don't necessarily think are about Teal'c, or about Mitchell. That's one of the things about being an actor, you're carrying this story with you. Your moments of revelation may occur in places where no one really expected it. Then the audience will pick it for themselves in context. What's a really important Mitchell moment could be a single scene in an episode which is otherwise carried by someone else entirely."

One episode does stand out in the thread that is Mitchell's first year as a part of *Stargate SG-1*, however, and that's the controversial story of 'Collateral Damage'. Not only does it show Mitchell apparently engaged in the murder of a woman, but it also reveals a small glimpse of anxiety from the character's past — a character who, up until that point, had seemed almost entirely free from negative emotional baggage. For Browder, discovering another, darker side to Mitchell was of no real surprise at all. "I think that most people do have that darker side," says Browder. "There is a tendency to view dark and broody as interesting, but generally speaking it's not the case. Often you'll find that people who have a sunny disposition have as interesting and as tortured a life as people with a dark disposition. It's more a case of, how do you take it on board, and how do you integrate it into your behavior in the outside world? We have a choice to either succumb to our darkness or not. And all of us, every single one of us, can look back at our life and pick those moments where, 'Gosh, that was horrible.' The question is, how do you wear it on the outside at the end of the day? We have a tendency to interpret an upbeat thing as being shallow, not serious, and only those things which are serious and dark deserve our attention. Particularly when we are young, we fall for this — 'Wow, they're tortured, they're dark, they're interesting.' And they're not! Their lives are no more interesting than the people who seem to lead happy lives. There are certain authors and artists who would disagree with me, because they use their darkness as their form of art. But, quite frankly, the joyful experience that we have as human beings is as enduring, and as artistically worthy, as the darkness that we have."

Browder remains pleased with the role, and admits that he likes his character and feels there is plenty more to learn about Mitchell. In fact, as far as Browder is concerned, the gradual discovery of Mitchell's personality and what he brings to the team is one of the most successful aspects of the character in season nine, as is the variety of actors he has had the opportunity to work with. "I like working with all the characters," the actor says. "Some of it translates to wanting to work with the actors. I loved the stuff I got to do with Chris, and Michael as well! There's stuff I would love to do with Landry... and all of them I guess. There is a sense about [season nine] that you're only beginning to define the relationships. These people are just getting to know each other, and that's an important thing, these people are getting to know each other as the audience is getting to know him." Å

Lieutenant Colonel Samantha Carter

"This is the best we have. I can get you a toaster if you need it."

For actress Amanda Tapping, *Stargate SG-1*'s ninth year on air began in a significantly different fashion to any other that had gone before it. Tapping was a new mother, having given birth to her daughter Olivia just as the season began filming, and thus did not return as Carter until the episode 'Beachhead'. Having spent the previous eight years as an integral and very prominent part of the SG-1 team, coming into a cast that had already been filming for several weeks — and which was significantly different — was an odd experience.

"It was an interesting season for me, because I came into it a bit later and it felt like it took me a while to find my feet," she explains. "It does still feel like *Stargate SG-1*, it's just a 'supersized' *Stargate SG-1*! Part of what makes [the show] so successful is its ability to have this incredibly interconnected tapestry that the writers have woven. It's so intense, so multi-layered — you pull one thread out and there's still a hundred threads holding the piece together, but every thread is unique. That's a gift that our writers have given us, and I think that this new storyline is just continuing on the exact same thing. I thought, once we'd got rid of the Goa'uld, 'Okay, we're pretty much done, the story's over. It's all good — end the show and move on.' But they pulled this out, which is pretty incredible."

One of the major new threads added by the writers in season nine was, of course, a new evil for SG-1 to battle in the form of the Ori. As far as Tapping is concerned, the religious overtones used by the writers to form this new danger to the galaxy is very closely — and cleverly — connected to the current larger world view. "Not to get too hyper-political about it, but I think it's really an interesting mirror of our society," says Tapping, "what happens when fundamentalism takes over, and how fundamentalist religion of any bent rules by fear and intimidation. We're seeing it in society, close to home and far afield, and it's interesting that we're paralleling it with the Ori. It's all fear and intimidation, it's bullying. [The] aggressor comes in, takes over, makes the people scared, puts them in a position where they have no choice but to follow or they die. It's an interesting geo-political statement that we're making — or not making," she adds. "We're just pointing it up, I think. I don't know if our writers intended for it to be [that], or whether they had conceptualised this storyline and suddenly the world's global political scene mirrored it. We're in a position where it makes

a lot of sense [to be] doing this kind of storyline. It's not just an over-the-top Goa'uld, which is the same thing. Here, they're doing it on the basis of a very specific religious ideology that the people have to follow. I think it's very well done, and I think for us, too — once we've defeated the Goa'uld, where do you go? Something bigger, better, scarier and more potent. And people do believe in it. There is a god quality to [the Ori]. But are they really Ascended beings, or have they just found a way to have all the smoke and mirrors and bells and whistles, without actually having properly Ascended? Is Ascension really what we think it is? It raises a whole bunch of questions that could keep us going for years!"

Though the larger landscape of *Stargate SG-1* has changed, in Tapping's eyes the character of Samantha Carter returned to Stargate Command not so much an altered person, as a restored one. "It was about [her] coming back, and it was fitting in a way, because it parallels what was happening with me. She was off doing her thing at Area 51, ostensibly research and development, but also looking after Cassie. She came back to work maybe a little better balanced, not necessarily with a better attitude, but she came back ready. She stepped away from this thing that had consumed her for eight years and came back ready to work again, as opposed to questioning whether she was spending too much time at work."

Throughout season nine, Carter was the dedicated soldier that she had always shown herself to be. However, to Tapping's mind, she also regained a focus that had perhaps been waning over several previous seasons. "So much of what we dealt with in seasons seven and eight was about her personal life," the actress recalls, "which was important. But what changed [for season nine] is that she came back with a better head on her shoulders, in a healthier way. The character arc was all about work. It wasn't about her personal life. So I think we've just got a more work-oriented Carter, more focused, back to the scientist-soldier. She was out of her comfort zone for a while there, and now she's back to it, but I'd like to think she's back to it with a little more depth of soul. The experiences that she had, the situation with Pete, losing her father, all these emotionally heavy [events] — that was kind of a new side of Carter. She went and visited it, she got a deeper understanding of herself as a woman and now she comes back with all of that. It's tucked in her back pocket, kind of like what happens with us as women. We have experiences and they are carried with us. And I think that's what's happened to her. From the episodic point of view you didn't see her do that much. You didn't see a lot of storylines going on that focused on her, but she was there and she was doing her thing. She was Carter and she was much more settled, is what I'd like to think," she laughs. ⅄

Teal'c

"To resist the influence of others, knowledge of one's self is most important."

With so many changes to the cast line-up for season nine, the familiar faces of the existing SG-1 team became all the more important to viewers naturally not wanting the show to change completely. Chris Judge, who had played Teal'c since pilot episode 'Children of the Gods', now found the Jaffa warrior a huge symbol of continuity amid the dramatic new landscape, not to mention far closer to center stage than the character had ever been before. This was a move, says Judge, that was for him particularly refreshing. "We really got back to the team," says Judge, of the season nine dynamic. "Even how the shots are set up — it's really, truly a team. Whatever anybody said," the actor asserts candidly, "it always was O'Neill and *then* the team. So now it's become a more interactive group."

For Judge, this new group gave him a different dimension to play with as Teal'c, not simply from a story point of view, but also from how the scenes were structured. Whereas before, Teal'c was most often providing reaction to other characters around him, Judge says that season nine altered his involvement in the scripts, and allowed for Teal'c to expand beyond that role. "You got to explore your own actions rather that reacting to something that someone else was doing, and I enjoyed that," he says. "I enjoyed not reading a script and going, 'Okay, how do I think Rick is going to play this?' and then, 'What reactions can I have to play off that?' because that would be the focus. So as an actor, it does give you a lot more to explore, and probably from a better place."

That new exploration, for Teal'c, was, in season nine, as much about the progress of the new Jaffa nation as it was about his own role in its development. Finally free of Goa'uld oppression, his fellows still had an uneasy struggle on their hands to find peace and security of a different sort, and Teal'c found himself at the very heart of that struggle. For Judge, season nine further represented an opportunity to carve a new path for the character — this time as a gifted orator and political aide.

"It was something I hoped for," Judge confesses, "and I think it was just the right amount. I didn't want him to try to be the leader of the Jaffa nation, because that would have taken him too far away from the SGC. So it was perfect that the Ori came and I couldn't be there [on Dakara], because I had to fight them. I, along with Bra'tac, have kind of become a

liason between the SGC and the Jaffa nation. So I really enjoyed how that was remedied."

The events surrounding the development of the new nation's structure also gave Judge a chance to work with talented guest star Lou Gossett Jr, who came aboard for six episodes as Gerak. "One of the things that stands out is getting to work with Lou Gossett," the actor smiles. "I had known Lou for quite some time on a personal level, not on a profession-al level. To kind of meld those two [aspects], and to really be able to spend a lot of time with him and pick his brain about everything — the business, life — everything about it just really stands out for me."

Gerak also brought the threat of the Ori directly to Teal'c's door, as over the course of the season he was forced to see the ambitious Jaffa leader fatally indoctrinated by the Priors and their attempt to spread Origin to our galaxy. For Judge, the introduction of the Ori as a new villain to replace the Goa'uld was a masterstroke, turning *Stargate SG-1* in a new, darker, and very welcome direction.

"They are much darker, much more powerful. I think that was one of the reasons that the Goa'uld had to play less of a role, because they had gotten a bit cartoony," Judge admits candidly. "No disrespect to any of the actors that played them and no disrespect to anybody who wrote them. But it was time for a darker adversary. Especially, I think, looking at *Stargate: Atlantis*, and how dark their adversaries are. I think the Ori are a fantastic addition to the mythology of the show. To actually face an enemy that seems unbeatable — what a great jump-off point for stories!"

Though the Goa'uld were no longer the central worry either for Teal'c or for the rest of SGC, it was clear that they weren't simply going to disappear off the map. Anubis, Baal and others were still very much in evidence throughout the season, and for Judge, that's exactly how it should be. "As much as we've gone towards the Ori and as great as the Ori are, the Goa'uld will always be part of the threat of the show. Maybe not major players any more, but it's what ties us to the beginnings of the show. It's part of the mythology that always has to be there, and at least looked at occasionally. They haven't all been killed off. They're still around. So I like the Ba'al storyline."

The season also revealed new aspects of Jaffa culture and history in the form of the Sodan, a unique race of warriors never subject to Goa'uld oppression.

"They were great. I really enjoyed [working with] Tony Todd (Lord Haikon). I had known of Tony and had met him once years ago, so it was fun meeting him and just sitting down to talk. We had been up for different parts in the various *Star Treks* against each other, and it was great just to interact with him. He's a lovely man. I thought they were going to try and get rid of me!" Judge adds with a huge belly laugh, about the introduction of the Japanese-like Sodan. He jokes, "They were wonderful guys but I was glad to say goodbye! No — I would like Teal'c to have learned something from his interaction with the Sodan. Because it's Teal'c's history. They have always been this mythological race of Jaffa that he finally got to meet, so I hope he is able to take something away from that, be it the technology, their frame of reference, or their fighting skills. Whatever it is, I would like to incorporate some of the Sodan stuff into Teal'c's own character." Å

Vala Mal Doran

"That's funny, isn't it? Daniel always wanted to get into my pants, and now I'm in his."

"Vala is irritating, but I think she's also interesting," says Claudia Black. "I'm enjoying seeing the layers peel back for this character, to see what the real vulnerabilities are underneath."

Having first appeared in the season eight episode 'Prometheus Unbound', Black's roguish former Goa'uld host had charmed both viewers and cast alike. Charmed them so much, in fact, that all were eager to see her return, and when star Amanda Tapping announced that she would be unavailable for the beginning of season nine, it left a temporary gap in the SG-1 line-up ideal for Vala to step into. It didn't hurt that Black had previously starred alongside leading man Ben Browder in cult sci-fi hit *Farscape*, and thus knew how to shoot science fiction television and already had her own dedicated fanbase!

"I got a test drive," the actress jokes of her early guest spot. "They expressed all along that they would love to have me full time if it was possible somehow, and the opportunity came up to just have me do at least a six episode arc. I knew that it would be a pleasant experience, and that always helps performance-wise. I remember one of the producers said to me on the phone before I accepted the gig, 'You know, you don't get a show running for nine years unless it's a happy show.' So it was an interesting experience, to come and see something that is such a well-oiled machine. It's been going for long enough that it knows what it is."

What was less well known, of course, was the character of Vala. Though it was clear that Claudia Black herself would slide into the show's line-up perfectly, and the writers and fans had enjoyed the character's interactions in 'Prometheus Unbound', expanding her from a guest to a full, three-dimensional role was important, particularly for the actress.

"She runs the risk of being a one-trick pony," Black asserts, of Vala's ability to laugh and be laughed at. "She can't just be a girl with a punchline. I think the most important thing is always to grow and develop, to make sure that your character has depth and, obviously, the potential to continue entertaining. It's important for Vala to have layers and levels of complexity. I think that she operates in a very childish way on a superficial level, but she's had to survive a lot. She has been damaged. A good liar always keeps as close to the truth as possible, so I would say a lot of the time when she is talking about what's happened to her, most of it would be true."

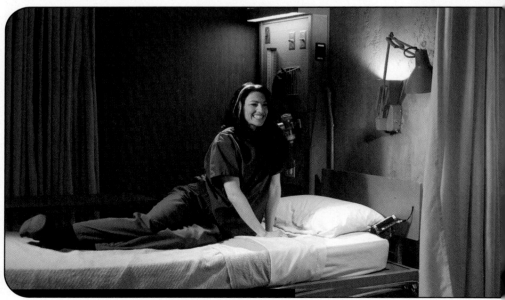

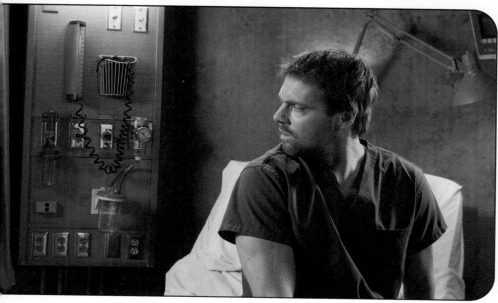

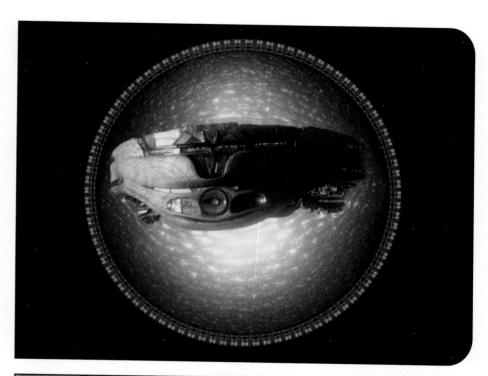

Emotional vulnerabilities aside, the audience got a very clear glimpse of Vala's physical vulnerabilities in the second part of the season opener, 'Avalon', when she undergoes a trial by fire. "I really didn't think they would go that far with it, I was actually very impressed," recalls the actress. "In terms of the story-telling, I was very impressed that they took that risk and they took it that far. It's rare to be surprised in television these days. That's when I started to feel as if I was edging more into the Aeryn territory, when things were getting a bit more tragic and serious,"

says Black, speaking of her character from *Farscape*. "But it's a welcome texture and shade to her as well.

"I don't suppose Dan Shea mentioned that he caught on fire when he was standing by the side of that," she adds, laughing. "It's always great when the stunt coordinator catches alight!"

Another striking aspect to Vala's early appearances as part of the *Stargate SG-1* team were her costumes, which in themselves courted controversy quite regularly. The actress reveals that she too was unsure about the raunchy style of some of them, particularly the leather fetish-style outfit that Vala first arrived wearing. "In the first episodes she is a Barbie doll. When [costume designer] Christine Mooney showed me her original designs, I wasn't too sure about it. I said, 'I really don't see her like that, I don't think that defines her. I don't see her as this hardcore leather bondage chick.' And I'd spent the past four or five years in leather anyway! It was just something that I thought she'd stolen. And I went and I talked to Rob [Cooper] about it and I said, 'I really don't think this is hers.'" After discussing a few different ideas for where the costume could have come from, Black jokingly suggested, "'Oh, I had a costume party last night and I didn't have time to change.' He liked that line, and gave me a whole paragraph riff on it! I said, 'But I didn't expect you to actually write that!' and he said, 'What an entrance line!'" Eventually though, the actress's wish for her wardrobe was realized. "I wanted to see her ability to adapt to every situation, and that is reflected in her costumes. I know they enjoyed it in the end, being able to do different ones for her."

Vala's costumes weren't the only aspect of her that evolved as the actress settled into her six-episode arc. As the writers got to know her beyond a one-episode guest spot, Vala extended herself to become a true, three-dimensional, embedded member of the team. "I said to Rob Cooper when he was directing — which was a lovely experience, by the way, Rob was really terrific to work with — I said, 'Wouldn't it be funny if Vala blah blah blah...' and in the second episode of season ten, that is exactly the B-storyline. But that's always the way the show goes. The writers are waiting for the actors to do something with the material, and the actors are waiting for the material from the writers. I was just really lucky that from the beginning with 'Prometheus Unbound' it was very obvious that Vala is a cheeky character. She's a naughty little minx and everyone enjoys writing for her, so most of the time I find that the writers give Vala very rich material to play with, and therefore give me very rich material to work with." Å

Recurring Characters

"I wish to meet this Prior of the Ori. If he preaches faith in false gods, then that is a concern for all of us. I wish to hear his claims, and challenge him."

After a memorable seven years leading SG-1 through many off-world adventures, and an eighth manning the fort at Stargate Command, General Jack O'Neill took a back seat for season nine, as actor **Richard Dean Anderson** decided that it was time to step away from the show. Listing Jack O'Neill as a recurring character seems odd given the character's huge influence on the series. However, even though O'Neill did not appear in every episode of the season, his presence was still firmly felt. A friend of the incoming General Hank Landry, viewers saw that O'Neill was still very influential in all things to do with Stargate Command. Whether he was sharing a beer with Landry or influencing Lieutenant Colonel Carter's eventual return to SG-1, it was clear that O'Neill wasn't going anywhere. As for Anderson, the actor who had given so much to the character for so long, he would never completely detach himself from the show, in the same way that he would never quite abandon the other long-running television series for which he is so well known, *MacGyver*. In between raising his young daughter and building a new house, and agreeing to star in a 'Mac'-themed episode of *The Simpsons* ('Kiss Kiss, Bang Bangalore'), Anderson made small appearances in the opening three-part story 'Avalon Part I' and 'II', and 'Origin'. As a handover to the new team, it couldn't have been a better gesture, and it also ensured that the name of O'Neill would continue to be as connected to the SG-1 team as possible.

A completely new face in the semi-regular line-up came in the form of actress **Lexa Doig**, playing the role of Stargate Command's new Chief Medical Officer, Dr Carolyn Lam. *Stargate SG-1* had been lacking a regular person in this position since the death of Janet Fraiser in season seven's 'Heroes, Part I', and it was thought high time that the infirmary was permanently staffed once more. Lam arrived with her own curious past — being, in fact, the estranged daughter of General Landry himself. In an echo of this family connection, in reality Doig is married to show star Michael Shanks, the couple having met during Shanks' guest role on *Andromeda*, a show in which Doig played regular dual character Rommie/Andromeda.

"I had no expectations of actually getting the part," Doig confesses. "I thought it would work against me that I'm Michael's wife, and I believe Michael actually went up to the production [office] after I was cast and said to Rob Cooper, 'Are you nuts? You hired my wife!'" the actress says with a laugh. "In the audition, I did the part and Rob Cooper looked at me and said, 'I'm just trying to figure out how you could be Beau Bridges' daughter.' I made a really politically incorrect comment about Vietnam — 'You know, he's a soldier, he's in 'Nam...' — and it's very funny, because that's actually the character's back story! I just thought it was very comic, because it was a very politically incorrect comment! And for that reason I kind of expected to get the part!"

Wanting to provide as much of a connection as possible to the previous seasons of *Stargate SG-1*, the producers turned to recurring character Walter

Harriman, played by **Gary Jones**. Having originally started life as a tiny bit-part character manning the monitors in Stargate Command, Canadian-born stand-up comedian Jones had, over the years, caught the attention of both the producers and the viewers (who lovingly dubbed him 'Chevron Guy') enough to become a very firm member of the team. First he got a name (Davis), then it got changed (to Harriman), and then, for season nine, Harriman got promoted to Chief Master Sergeant. As a familiar face that had traveled through the years (though not through the gate itself) with the original team, the technician was a welcome familiarity and, as such, found his horizons expanded as never before with the latest season. In 'Avalon, Part I', Harriman has the distinction of being the first member of Stargate Command to welcome the somewhat bemused Colonel Mitchell to his new post. Throughout the season, moreover, Harriman became much more than simply the guy that said "Chevron seven locked", quickly establishing himself as a right-hand man to General Landry. With his responsibilities becoming more involved as the

season progressed, it could surely not be long before Chief Master Sergeant Walter Harriman stepped through the gate for the first time... though it wouldn't happen during season nine.

With the turbulent unfurling of the new Jaffa nation and its attendant politics came the addition of another new semi-regular character, though one who would not last long. A determined leader at odds with Bra'tac and Teal'c, Gerak would fall foul of the Ori's promise of power and become a Prior, and though he would eventually decide to do the right thing and save his people from more slavery, Gerak would not survive the struggle. Played by Oscar-winning actor **Lou Gosset Jr**, Gerak's short-lived sojourn as part of *Stargate SG-1* nonetheless became one of the most memorable guest-turns the show had entertained in its entire history. Gosset, a friend of show star Chris Judge, had actually been intrigued by the part of Landry, which had been offered to both him and Beau Bridges simultaneously. After various discussions, Gerak was created instead, and the producers welcomed their most prestigious guest turn yet. Appearing in five episodes of season nine, Gosset brought a dignity and weight to the role, and a fascinating expansion of the saga of the Jaffa people's quest for freedom.

Just when you thought it was safe to visit the snakes at the zoo, the Goa'uld reappeared to cause havoc in the wake of their lost empire. Or at least one of them did... Well, one Goa'uld and his clones. System Lord Ba'al, as was, first appeared in sixth season episode 'Abyss', a particularly nasty piece of work with a penchant for torture. Played by South African actor **Cliff Simon**, Ba'al was another, less pleasant, link to *Stargate SG-1*'s origins, and the stubborn parasite wasn't about to lose his empire quietly. Ensconcing himself on Earth, and producing a few dozen clones to complicate matters, Ba'al ensured that he would cause plenty of trouble for the SG-1 team. Actor Simon was certainly surprised to discover that Ba'al's downfall in season eight episode 'Reckoning' wasn't the end of his journey with *Stargate SG-1*. But, as everyone knows, no one really dies in science fiction — particularly if you're an ancient parasite with a penchant for science.

Another familiar face to return for season nine was **Tony Amendola**, reprising his much-loved role as Teal'c's mentor, Master Bra'tac. Unsurprisingly, Bra'tac proved to be the voice of reason amongst the political confusion reigning on Dakara — although politics was the last vocation the warrior was expecting to find himself taking up, as the veteran actor explains. "He's been forced to be a more political animal. He was of a warrior class, and now as the hunger for freedom and democracy [has grown], he has necessarily had to put that to the side and participate in a political arena that he doesn't always necessarily understand very well. He's prone to more errors than he was when he was a warrior, I think," says the actor.

Amendola had no problem with showing the more vulnerable, less confident side of Bra'tac. "It has to grow and change over the course of years," the actor says. "There was a strong sense of trying to pass on the mantel with Teal'c. It's when the student surpasses the master, and trying to mark that."

Despite his humility and occasional lack of surety in his new position, the character has retained the integrity and spiritual nature that has made him such a favorite amongst viewers — and provided another familiar face to carry on the tradition of *Stargate SG-1*'s past. Å

Stunts

Dan Shea

Diary: 'Beachhead'

So, they wanted to ratchet six people at a forty-five degree angle about thirty feet high in the air, for a distance of about sixty feet. Man from VFX would take them most of the way. Not a problem...

...The problem was that the lift that was supposed to be there, wasn't ('there' being the Richmond Sand Dunes, which is essentially the middle of nowhere). This was to have been used to move the incredibly heavy cement blocks which act as a stabilizer for the giant spreader bar. The spreader bar is the huge metal bar located high in the air and connected to the ratchet, whose purpose was to keep the stunt people separate as they were violently wrenched through the air, so they wouldn't plough into each other. So we had to use the gargantuan crane, which anchored the ratchets, to set the cement blocks.

The problem was, the gargantuan crane couldn't travel in sand. So we had to put thin pieces of plywood underneath the crane to travel it. Then, as the pieces of plywood started to get crushed, we dropped the cement anchors as deep into the sand as possible because we thought the crane would get stuck and that would be bad.

The problem was the cement blocks were parallel to the spreader bar, and they needed to be upstage of the spreader bar to provide a better anchor.

But, whatever, we've already wasted four hours. Time to move on...

It was a beautiful sunny day, and every conceivable stunt person had come out to play with us. What's the old joke? How do you get ten stunt guys out to set? Hire one! Well, I had hired six, and we had an acre of pads for them to lie on and sun themselves while they networked.

Do we need an ambulance standing by? It seemed pretty safe; there were tons of pads. But a wire could conceivably wrap around a finger or a neck. So, ambulance it was.

Opposite: A Prior prepares for his close-up during the filming of 'Beachhead'.

By the time we actually hooked the stunt people up for a ride, it was lunch. Funny thing about being in the middle of nowhere, there's no catering, no craft service, and everyone was starving. But we had to keep going. We had ratcheted a bunch of sand bags already to simulate the weight of humans being pulled, but every time, the bags got

Above: One of the most difficult stunts of the season — Vala burning in 'Avalon, Part II'.

dragged really slowly through the sand. And guess what? When we yanked the humans, they too looked like they were being dragged really, really slowly. This was hardly a good demonstration of the power of the Ori!

The problem was, the spreader bar wasn't anchored properly. We were losing all of our power on every pull. So we had to crank up the power!

The problem was, the total shock load allowed on this particular crane was 1800lbs, and we had already exceeded that with only three guys on the wires! We still had three more stunt players to hook up! With that kind of potential shock load, we could destroy the crane! (Or maybe I'm being overly dramatic...) The crane guy wanted to reconfigure everything. But that could just wind up wasting another eight hours and we could be right back where we started — and we shoot tomorrow morning at 6am. So we decided to put one more stunt guy on the wire and blast them and see what happened. Luckily, nothing happened! The shock load for four guys was no different than with three. I think that's

Above: A large explosion in 'Stronghold', courtesy of Don Shea...

physically impossible, but I guess hurtling through the air is not an exact science... So, we decided to ratchet all six guys (actually, five guys and one girl). And it worked great! And the crane wasn't destroyed! So we shut everything down and ate. We ate a lot. Except for the stunt guys. They ate a moderate amount. We couldn't have those guys bulking up and causing the crane to topple onto the crew.

The next day was beautiful! The actors were there! The crew was there! The media was there! The ambulance was there! Even more stunt guys were there! And, most importantly, craft service and catering were there! (I kept my stunt guys hooked up to the wire so they couldn't gorge themselves.) It was a butt-slapping, towel-snapping love-fest!

When the director yelled, "Action!" the Ori raised his staff and all six stunt rebel Jaffa flew at least forty feet through the air with the greatest of ease at a forty-five degree angle, for a distance of at least seventy feet. Up, up, up, into the deep blue sky. And if Mark from VFX has his way, they're still going...

No problem! Å

Make-Up Effects

Todd Masters

For make-up effects guru Todd Masters, the ninth season of *Stargate SG-1* brought some extraordinary challenges for his team. Despite having worked in television and films for many years and created numerous make-ups, 'Avalon, Part II' still provided Masters Inc with a real surprise when it came to the graphic nature of the effects they were asked to develop. "That was pretty surprising for *Stargate SG-1*," Masters admits. "I'm always fascinated when they stretch it and make it more than your average sci fi show. When I read that script, I couldn't believe it, I was like, 'Really?'" he laughs. "But I thought it worked well."

Though Masters and his team enjoyed creating as realistic an effect as possible, they were rather worried that the finished make-up was too over-the-top for a family television show. "That was a burn make-up that we did on a double of Vala," explains Masters. "We didn't actually do it on Claudia. It was a multi-layered prosthetic, face and hands, and we pushed it. It was funny, when we were in the meetings, we were saying, 'You know, the burn is pretty horrific. We can't really make a nice-looking burn! There's no friendly side to burns!' So we did it like it was written, and we imagined what would happen with that kind of body burn. So it's pretty horrific, and it's based on real evidence."

Even though the effects were created on a double of Claudia Black, the actress was going to put herself as close to the fire as possible. So, to get a good match, and so that the director could cut from Black to her double as late as possible, Masters and his team wanted to get the likeness of the prosthetics as close to Black as they could. "What we did was, with the life cast of the actress's face, we put it onto the double, so we actually had her features on the double. It looked just like her. There was a slight expression in the face — it was a prosthetic, so it had to move — we made the eyes kind of opened, and one of them was severely charred. We actually made a little piece on the eye that they could edit, whether or not they thought it was too much or too little. I think ultimately they took it off because it was a bit horrific! So it was prosthetics that look like her and was gouged into and had layers of charred peeling flesh. It's a matter of basically taking the sculpture and creating the image."

However, not only did the team have to create the illusion of badly charred skin, they also had the challenge of the regeneration, a reversal back into the healthy body of Claudia Black. "We did it in different

Above: Too horrific for Stargate SG-1? *Masters' most controversial make-up for the show.*

stages. So we would put the make-up on and shoot a little bit," explains Masters. "Those are generally done as second-unit pieces so that you can take some time with them and make sure they are positioned correctly. It was tricky. We did it the way we used to do it back in the day," he laughs, "the old 'werewolf' transformation!"

Another major aspect of season nine was the development of the Priors and their distinctive — and disturbing — make-up. "The initial design came out of the art department. Typically, we work with the art department and they will develop certain ideas for new characters and we will realize it," says Masters, describing the process. "They usually sketch out the design, and we make it into the real thing. The art department has been really fantastic about supplying designs. They're not make-up artists, but they come across with an overall design that goes throughout the show, so we need to go into that whole river of thought. For the most part we do match their ideas. We do our own designs as well, but we really share the duties of the design. Since they're in the production office and they've got Brad Wright and Robert Cooper and the producers [there], they can just cross the hallway and see what they think."

With the Priors, the producers and art department had a specific idea of how they wanted the make-up to look. "The idea was that these people had looked at the gods, or something like that," explains Masters. "So this whole concept that their eyes and their brows were very wrinkly continued that — they were oddly aged. So that was the whole conceit

Make-Up Effects

Above: *Arthur's Mantle fails, revealing the face of Volnek, transformed into a murderous monster by a Prior.*

of the wrinkly eye area. We did Photoshops on the first actors, and after a while we moved right into creating the prosthetics."

Helping Masters to create the Priors was his small Vancouver-based effects team, including Sarah Pickersgill and Brad Procter.

"Basically, everything starts with a life cast of the actor," Pickersgill explains. "So we started with one of those and we sculpted on with clay what the pieces were actually going to look like. So, for the Priors, we sculpted on a brow and some cheek pieces to kind of hollow out the eyes, and added crow's feet around the eyes so it was all wrinkly. And then what we do is take a mould of that sculpture and eventually pour in whatever material we would use. So foam latex or gelatin, or whatever medium we are going to use. The Priors were a relatively simple make-up, which was fortunate," she laughs, "because sometimes we didn't have much time. They would call on a Friday and say, 'We need a Prior on Monday.'"

It was important for the realism of the characters that each new actor have his face cast and prosthetic applications created specifically for his features, particularly for the Prior make-up, which was thinner than other applications for the series. "Where people's lines begin are different," says Pickersgill, "and we try to have the appliance blend into their natural lines." Procter elaborates, "For example, if a character's got crow's feet, and the actor also has crow's feet that match, that helps us line up the piece."

The Prior prosthetic itself started off as a rather delicate application, using gelatin as the basis of the make-up pieces molded for the actors. "The Priors we began doing in gelatin," says Pickersgill, "just because it's got a nice translucency to it — it's kind of like skin. But we had a lot of trouble, because we were shooting a lot of the Priors in a hot studio. It was in the summer, and suddenly the gelatin began to melt with the sweat! So our on-set people were not very happy," she laughs. "We ended up changing it for something else and doing them in foam latex."

Changing to foam latex solved the problem, although it did mean creating a slightly different look for the Priors. "The nice thing about gelatin," explains Procter, "is that you can pigment it so it has the same translucent properties as skin. Some of the person's skin will show through so it's easier to match, and if it's side-lit, it actually looks like flesh. With foam, it's solid; it doesn't have the light transmission. It photographs very well, but you need the camera there to supply the trick. Whereas with really well done gelatin make-up, someone could just walk in, have a conversation with you and you wouldn't even notice [it], necessarily. Even a very well colored [foam] piece still doesn't have the light transmission properties."

"It seems like we do that a lot," says Masters of the evolving make-up. "We'll do little things. That's the great thing about doing a show for so long, you get to really refine the make-up design and techniques." Λ

Above: The Priors — one of the most delicate make-ups accomplished for season nine.

Visual Effects: In-House

Michelle Comens

or Michelle Comens, *Stargate SG-1*'s ninth year brought a fair amount of challenges in terms of visual effects, as well as a new in-house department to oversee. With the visual effects output increasing every year, especially since the addition of the effects-heavy spin-off, *Stargate: Atlantis*, it seemed prudent to establish a department actually on the Bridge Studios lot. Whilst still using vendors such as Rainmaker, Image Engine, Atmosphere and Spin, Michelle Comens' own on-set department would create many of the effects themselves, reducing the show's reliance on external effects houses.

"It's been a huge undertaking to have a full in-house department here and we've had some growing pains," she laughs, "but it really seems to be working out and gelling together. We've always had a matte painter in-house, which has been so helpful, and at the end of the year we usually keep our playback department on to do some compositing jobs for us — so it's just been on a really small scale [before].

"It's hard for the [vendors]. They still get a tremendous amount of work from us, but not really huge numbers. Especially the last episode ['Camelot'], because we always do such a huge end of season, and the vendors that I usually work with didn't work on it. They're getting a smaller portion of it. But they understand, and it's necessity, really. If the show is going to keep going, it has to find ways to make it feasible, especially with the [Canadian] dollar being so strong now. This way, we get better value for our show, and we're going to get better and better."

Rather than dividing her time between *Stargate SG-1* and *Stargate: Atlantis*, for season nine Comens concentrated only on the parent show. James Tichenor, who had worked as visual effects supervisor on *Stargate SG-1* since the show's beginning up until the end of season seven, returned to supervise *Stargate: Atlantis*' second season. "This year it's been great, because James Tichenor is supervising on *Stargate: Atlantis*, and then Mark Savela is alternating between both shows. That's just been awesome. I'd never really worked with Mark like this before. We used to work with him years ago, but not on this show. He's introduced me to working with new vendors that I hadn't really worked with before."

The new look of *Stargate SG-1* in season nine gave the visual effects department a chance to try out some new techniques and develop some different signature effects for the series. In particular, the Earth's new

Above: An Ori ship, in full 'Crusade' mode.

enemy, the Ori, made for a whole slew of new virtual components. "That's one nice thing actually," she says. "Over the years we often work with the same vendors and the same artists. A lot of the people that we have now are new. Sometimes it's hard when they're working on something that has an established look, but when it's something new, they come up with something really creative that I would never have thought of. So it's the guys playing with the tools they have on their computers, coming up with stuff and seeing if this is what the producers like. It's also been a little bit hard because we're doing a lot of stuff that's beginning to become part of the bible for the show."

Some of those 'bible' components included the massive Ori ships, designed by concept artist James Robbins and realized by artists under Comens' supervision. The team also had to come up with new effects for the Ori weapons discharge, something sufficiently different to what had been seen over the nine years previously. "Our first stab [was] kind of like a beam with a gaseous vibe to it, which is something that we've never really done before," says Comens, describing how the effect evolved to its final look. "What we designed for the weapon didn't really work for a battle, so we came up with a secondary weapon. Things like that naturally develop when you have to tell the story."

Aside from finding an all new look for the Ori threat, there were several other huge visual effects episodes for the team to tackle throughout season nine. One particularly intensive episode was 'Ripple Effect'. "That,

Above: The destruction of the Prometheus.

for me, was definitely one of the highlights of the season," says Comens. "We did 'Gemini' the year before, and that went well. But when the full script [for 'Ripple Effect'] came out I was like, 'Oh my goodness!' Luckily it was Stephen [Bahr] and I doing it — we had done 'Gemini' together before, so we had some experience.

"The first day on set, the first thing we did was a motion control shot, which is a big camera with a repeatable head on a repeatable track. So you can move your shots and do multiple passes. So we started, and basically we had to twin the whole cast. Which doesn't sound hard... but you have a moving camera, you have a cast that are in one position that all have to move into another position when their twins come in... It was a very ambitious episode," Comens laughs. "It was hard for everybody, all of it. Then there was the system we were using, which we had never worked with before. On 'Gemini' we did a thing called Hot Gears which had a repeatable head, but this was a repeatable head *and* track. It was this whole thing that was taking a lot longer than we thought. And believe it or not, that is so hard to shoot. Because with a lot of stuff, we just fix it in post. If you don't shoot it right, we can just fix it. But if you don't shoot this right, there's nothing you can do. The actors are there, and if the eyeline's not right, if they're occupying the wrong space, if something has moved — there are so many things that can't be fixed, so it was a challenge. Steve and I were there twelve hours a day the whole

time, because it was just so intense. We needed each other for another set of eyes. But it was good. Peter DeLuise was great. By the end he got us all working really well with it! But the first couple of days were hard."

Another episode that provided a new set of challenges for the team was 'The Scourge', the script for which called for millions of bugs — all of which were created by visual effects. "I hadn't really worked with Ken Girotti, the director of that, before," Comens explains. "It was interesting, he had a different way of shooting, different ideas. It's good, it's nice to work with different people. James Robbins designed those [bugs], and then we got one of our vendors, Image Engine, who have done all our other bugs like the Replicators, to do them. We talked about scale and how big they should be, because the volume of them is so huge and we hadn't ever done that many bugs, so that was a whole new thing."

As often happens on episodes involving many visual effects, it isn't just a case of adding the CG elements in after a scene has been shot. Instead, the scene needs to have certain physical elements added to it during shooting to make the visual elements added later meld properly with the rest of the action. In the case of 'The Scourge', one particular requirement stated in the script — that a column of bugs would erupt out of the soil — proved insurmountably difficult. "That went out of the script before we got to set," Comens admits. "There were some things that just weren't possible. Usually [the] special effects [department] can totally handle that

Above: *We've got Carters! A scene from the filming of 'Ripple Effect'.*

kind of stuff — they'll just dig a hole, fill it up, and then they can do anything! But we were filming out at a rock quarry, where you can't dig! So it was a little bit tricky, but we came up with a new way of doing it. On the day we didn't have time to shoot what we wanted, so it's a whole different effect. Joe [Mallozzi] and Paul [Mullie], the writers/producers, came up with that. It was a good solution — it worked out really cool."

Season nine also featured some spectacular space-battles, far more visually intensive than anything accomplished on *Stargate SG-1* before. One was the destruction of the *Prometheus* in latter season episode 'Ethon'. "Robert Cooper had a real vision for that, so that made it easy because he had very fixed shots in mind," Comens explains. "He recommended certain movies we should look at. That really helps, when you've got a producer that's written something like that, that he's explained it to you. It's easier to get the vision in your head. The rough animation is the key to having that bang on. A lot of times, if we're lucky enough, we'll get James Robbins in the art department to do [storyboards] as well, and that really helps. He's so great to work with."

The biggest effects sequence of the season by far, however, was the climactic final battle as the Ori fleet invades our galaxy in 'Camelot'. "We have Ori ships firing at a mothership, and two *Daedalus*-class ships. And then we have the Lucian Alliance come in with more motherships, and we have an Asgard ship in there, and they're all taking a beating from the

Ori ships. Reading the script it was hard to picture it all in your head because there's so much going on," Comens says with a laugh. "But it was great because when we first sat down, the director [Martin Wood] was awesome. He tore up pieces of cardboard, wrote the names of the ships on those and then put them all over the table, and put in a Supergate, and walked it all through with us! Everybody had to get, spatially, how it was going to happen, and then we could see, 'Oh, we can get the cameras in here and in here.' After getting that worked out, it was good.

"It's a humungous space battle and I don't think we've ever done such a long space battle with so many ships, so much going on," adds Comens. "We couldn't really split it off with different people doing different things, because it all blends together. It was a lot for an in-house department."

Ultimately, however, having an in-house department has revolutionized *Stargate SG-1*'s visual effects — even if Comens herself has to be strict about her involvement! "It's sometimes hard because you don't want to leave! You feel you should be there the whole time," she laughs. "But for the most part it's good. I find it easier to really set out what I want, then just leave them to it and then come back, so that you're not looking over their shoulders constantly. Everyone can kind of get muddled up that way — you kind of need a fresh pair of eyes. And our producers are great, too. They're close as well, so if we really need feedback straight away we can usually get it. It keeps everything going, which we have to do." Λ

Above: *Chris Judge lights up the set during the filming of 'Camelot'.*

Bruce Woloshyn

The offices of Rainmaker Studios are unobtrusive despite their size — a whitewashed block building in an industrial area not far from downtown Vancouver, BC. Looking at the outside, no one would guess that the building is home to one of the most respected post-production laboratories and visual effects houses in North America. Step inside Rainmaker's plush, maze-like offices, however, and it's a different matter entirely. Having worked on thousands of projects in their long-running history, Rainmaker has collected a huge number of movie posters, which proudly adorn the many winding corridors within.

Rainmaker's association with *Stargate SG-1* began in the show's first season, when they started handling post-production and visual effects work for the show. In fact, in a specially temperature controlled vault in the building's basement, Rainmaker still houses all the original negatives from the early seasons of *Stargate SG-1* — including the single master tape produced for 'Children of the Gods'!

Bruce Woloshyn, Rainmaker's visual effects supervisor, has worked with the studio since its earliest days, and Rainmaker as it is now has its history rooted in another well-established company. "Rainmaker was originally founded in 1979, as a company called Gas Town Post and Transfer, by Larry Meerhead, Bob Campbell and Peter Sara," Woloshyn explains. "They started the post[-production] facility that did film transfers and editing, etcetera. In 1994, Bob Scarabelli, a former employee of Gas Town Post and Transfer, decided he wanted to start a visual effects company in Vancouver. He came to Vancouver, bought a couple of very big computers, and acquired some space from Gas Town so he had somewhere to start up. That's about when he phoned me."

Woloshyn, a Canadian born in Saskatchewan, had started his career as an editor before moving into the growing industry of computer animation. The first television series that the artist turned his talents to was another cult audience favorite — *Highlander*. "I got a phone call at home one night," he says. "I'd never met Bob, but I knew who he was. I was living in Seattle at the time, and he said that he wanted to do this and would I be interested? We knew that for Rainmaker, we were going to need a film laboratory, editing facilities, and all these other things that Gas Town already had. So, instead of going somewhere else and building our own stuff, we merged the two companies."

As a result, although Rainmaker in its current incarnation has only been around since 1994, the company's components have a much further-reaching history — in fact going back twenty-seven years, to when Gas Town originally began. That vast store of experience is what has helped make Rainmaker such a force to be reckoned with in the world of post-production and animation effects, and also what has contributed to making *Stargate SG-1's* past decade of visual effects so stunning.

Above: *"You can actually see the fluctuations in the event horizon"…*

"The very first year that we had Rainmaker was the pilot of *Stargate SG-1,*" Woloshyn recalls of the studio's early involvement with the show. "We got in right at the beginning. It was the second television series that I ever worked on when I came here. We were involved from a post-production standpoint right from day one for *Stargate SG-1,* because we had done other MGM shows that had been produced here in Vancouver."

Though Rainmaker started out handling all the post-production for the series, it soon became clear that the show would also need help with the intensive visual effects that became *Stargate SG-1's* hallmark. The Stargate 'puddle', the Jaffa staff weapon blasts, the transporter rings — all of these were developed for television by Rainmaker, from designs by the show's concept artists.

With the growth of the show and the addition of the spin-off, *Stargate: Atlantis,* in recent years, *Stargate SG-1* began to contract work out to additional effects houses in and around Vancouver. "The way it's worked

Above: *Before: no, not some weird* Stargate SG-1 *cast initiation ceremony...*

for years on the show — with the exception of the *Stargate: Atlantis* start up — is that MGM hires its own [on set] visual effects supervisors," Woloshyn explains. "So they had their own supervisors, like Michelle [Comens]. Michelle will get a script, break it down, create a budget, and determine from that what shots are going to be visual effects. She will then contact the vendors that work on the show — us, Image Engine, Spin — and ask us all to bid. We do that, and shots are awarded to the various vendors based on all kinds of things: experience, whether you've done that kind of work before, what they're comfortable with, price — like any other kind of subcontractor."

Over the years, Rainmaker's experience at dealing with certain *Stargate SG-1* visual components has become unsurpassable. At the show's beginning, however, even these were incredibly complicated. "The longer we're on the air, the more efficient we get at doing signature effects for *Stargate SG-1*. I remember when we were developing a puddle pass-through ten years ago — it took us days and days to do one, which is why you only saw one or two! The better and faster we got at it, the cheaper they became and the more we did. Something that used to take us three days to do, you can sometimes now do in three hours. Staff blasts were a big deal way back when, but by seasons five or six, I would do an entire staff blast sequence by myself — just because it was easy and I needed a rest," says Woloshyn with a laugh. "It was fun to do, it always

looked cool and it didn't require a lot of work."

With the advent of *Stargate: Atlantis*, which is even more visual effects-intensive than its parent show, Rainmaker has turned most of its attention to creating that show's environment and effects. For *Stargate SG-1*'s season nine, however, Rainmaker did provide several sequences and various background effects — some of which viewers might not even notice without being told of their existence. "Sometimes we add things in there that you wouldn't know we'd added," says Woloshyn, using a shot from the episode 'Prototype' as an example. "Here comes our guy that's supposed to be Anubis. He's trying to escape, he walks up to the elevator shaft. He uses his mental powers to open the doors, and looks down the elevator shaft. But there is no elevator shaft!" Woloshyn says with a laugh. The set of the SGC, of course, is not built with huge elevator shafts inside. When someone opens the door of an elevator, they're actually looking down at a solid floor, with a green screen that the digital artists can replace. "This is a shot that nobody would think twice about, and it's actually a hard one to do, because when you open the doors, there's just nothing there. Practical, photographed things are almost more of a challenge to put together than something that's completely digital. If it's completely digital, you have control over everything. With [something like] this, we only have control over what we put in the hole. Part of what compositing is, is taking the things that don't work and making them so that they do. It's the little things. For

Above: ...And after: it's the transporter rings in action!

Above: *What would Stargate SG-1 be without some really big space ships?*

example, if the red lights are flashing in the practical photography, well, when you go and do it digitally, you have to make sure you put those little things in so that people buy into it. Everything that's put in with visual effects is a conscious decision. We don't have accidents. You sometimes have accidents that you incorporate, but that's another conscious decision — like when you put layers together, or something like that. But nothing's just there because it is — it's there because one of us thought to put it there!"

Despite spending much of their visual effects time *on Stargate: Atlantis*, Rainmaker still provides all the post-production work for *Stargate SG-1*. Every episode of the series passes through Rainmaker's hard drives. Footage first becomes 'dailies' — the regular portions of footage of each shooting day that the directors and producers view to gauge an episode's progress. These are either sent to the studio or viewed at Rainmaker's own in-house cinema (possibly accompanied by a beer or two from their comfortable on-premises pub!). Each day, more footage arrives to be viewed and also color corrected. Finally, the episode returns from *Stargate SG-1*'s own editors as a near-finished rough cut to be color corrected overall, and then again after the shots have finally been assembled, to have visual effects shots added into the spaces and be mixed for sound. After a few more tweaks here and there, the episode is ready for delivery to the SCI FI Channel for airing.

For Woloshyn, working on the *Stargate SG-1* franchise is like dealing with family. He and the Rainmaker crew have seen the show grow over

almost a decade, and the artist says that one of his sons learned to walk going up and down the Stargate's ramp. Woloshyn himself has appeared in numerous uncredited roles over the years, including the season nine finale 'Camelot', playing a character named Captain Gerald E. Jennings. And, as *Stargate SG-1* looks forward to more seasons on air with its new outlook, the show's relationship with Rainmaker Studios seems set to continue to be as close as it has ever been. Å

Above: *The wonders of technology.*

S eason ten! 200 episodes! Guinness Book of World Records! Wow! Quite an achievement. Oh wait, this is the season nine book, isn't it?

As I write this, we're hard at work shooting episode 203 and basking in the glow of all the press celebrating our overwhelming, tremendous success. It somehow seems wrong to have to rewind a whole year and talk about modest old season nine as though this year hasn't happened. All right, fine, I'll dial up the Stargate, slingshot around the sun during a solar flare and send myself back in time…

Season nine? Are you kidding me? Don't you people know an ending when you see one?! 'Reckoning'? 'Threads'? 'Moebius'? Not one, not two, but three epic endings neatly wrapping up the series that is *Stargate SG-1*. But no, apparently "The End" doesn't mean what I think it means. Of course if it did you wouldn't be reading this Afterword. Apparently, if there's more, you'll just keep right on going reading or watching as the case may be. Not that season nine is an Afterword. We like to think of it as much more of an "as well as".

But seriously folks, do you know how much time writing nine seasons of television takes? Now I have to write about all that writing on top of that. Please, give me a break. The fingertips of my middle two fingers are wearing out.

Okay, so maybe there are some of you who quit watching and are only reading this out of spite. (As if that makes sense.) Others continue watching only to complain, hoping to see the series die a slow and painful death, withering on the vine. "Why must it change?" you cried. "I want the old team back the way it was in the good seasons like one through three, going on adventures together, encountering cool alien bad guys like Hathor and Seth, the way it was meant to be!" Well, the fact is, nothing stays the same. Things die when they *don't* change. Maybe we lost some viewers when Richard packed up and went home to Malibu at the end of season eight but hey, look at that, we're still on the air. And he'll be back. I just *feel* it.

I'm sure many of you have heard how season nine was at one time supposed to be season one of a new series. If you hadn't heard, you're now up to speed. We even had a title: *Stargate Command*. Some observant fans (and what else might you be if you're reading a companion book about the show) might have caught Walter Harriman welcoming Colonel Mitchell to Stargate Command at the beginning of 'Avalon'. However, for various reasons a nondisclosure agreement does not permit me to discuss, the show continued on as *Stargate SG-1*. Some wittier and more sarcastic people than I said a better title would have been "*FarGate*" because of the addition of Ben Browder and Claudia Black to the cast. I honestly think that ceased to be an issue the moment we saw them inhabit their new characters. So, on with the new. New team, new Beau Bridges, new villains.

The irony is the new is much more like the old than the old was ever going to be going forward. We got some more money thanks to one of our biggest fans who also happens to pull the purse strings at the studio. His name is Charlie Cohen — or Saint Charlie, as we like to call him — and that extra little bit of cash made a world of difference. In fact, many worlds of difference. We could get out of the base, go out into the galaxy, even go to another galaxy and begin again. Yup, that's it for endings. Time to start fresh. Hey, you asked for it. I read the GateWorld.net poll that said fans were most interested in the history of the Ancients. Well, have some Ori then. And forget about series finales. I said to the audience at Comic-Con 2005, "If the show doesn't get picked up for season ten this will be the strangest series finale ever." Talk about a cliffhanger. Go on, talk about it. We knew it was a risk but we also knew if it worked it could mean the show might last a lot longer than just one more year. And if it didn't, hey, nine years could never be called a failure. Well, I'm sure some people could call it that but no one can debate that it's one tenth of a life-time… if your life is ninety years. Still, ten years would be nice. 200 episodes. Boy, I sure hope that happens.

Well, that about wraps it up for another Afterword. The word that comes after everything that's of any real importance. All that's left are the thanks. You are awesome! For those of you on the cast and crew skimming through this looking for some mention, a heartfelt shoutout that will in some small way provide you with a sense of personal validation, please substitute your name for the 'you' in the previous sentence. Then smile. Every day is a gift. Thanks to Sharon for writing all the important stuff. Thanks to my family for putting up with me, especially on the rare occasions when I let some of the crap we have to deal with get to me. I should never forget how spoiled and lucky I really am. Thanks to all the wonderful people who make working on the show as fun as it possibly could be. We wouldn't do it if we didn't like it a lot and of course we couldn't do it if you, the fans, didn't like it a lot. Thanks.

And now, if you'll excuse me, I hear history calling. Back to the future.

Robert C. Cooper
Vancouver, May 2006

CELEBRATE THE GATE!

CELEBRATE THE 10TH ANNIVERSARY OF STARGATE SG-1.
GET IN THE GATE AND UP TO SPEED WITH
THE ORIGINAL SERIES AS SEEN ON Sci Fi

PICK UP THE ALL NEW SLIM PACK DVDs IN STORES NOW